NANYANG

ISEAS YUSOF ISHAK
INSTITUTE

The **ISEAS – Yusof Ishak Institute** (formerly Institute of Southeast Asian Studies) is an autonomous organization established in 1968. It is a regional centre dedicated to the study of socio-political, security, and economic trends and developments in Southeast Asia and its wider geostrategic and economic environment. The Institute's research programmes are grouped under Regional Economic Studies (RES), Regional Strategic and Political Studies (RSPS), and Regional Social and Cultural Studies (RSCS). The Institute is also home to the ASEAN Studies Centre (ASC), the Nalanda-Sriwijaya Centre (NSC) and the Singapore APEC Study Centre.

ISEAS Publishing, an established academic press, has issued more than 2,000 books and journals. It is the largest scholarly publisher of research about Southeast Asia from within the region. ISEAS Publishing works with many other academic and trade publishers and distributors to disseminate important research and analyses from and about Southeast Asia to the rest of the world.

NANYANG

Essays on Heritage

WANG GUNGWU

ISEAS YUSOF ISHAK
INSTITUTE

First published in Singapore in 2018 by
ISEAS Publishing
30 Heng Mui Keng Terrace
Singapore 119614
E-mail: publish@iseas.edu.sg
Website: <http://bookshop.iseas.edu.sg>

ISEAS Library Cataloguing-in-Publication Data

Wang, Gungwu, 1930–
Nanyang : Essays on Heritage / by Wang Gungwu.
1. Chinese—Malaya.
2. Chinese—Singapore.
3. Peranakan (Asian people)—Malaya.
4. Chinese—Malaysia—Ethnic identity.
5. Chinese—Singapore—Ethnic Identity.
6. Malaysia—Relations—China.
7. Singapore—Relations—China.
I. Title.
DS595.2 C5W249   2018

ISBN 978-981-4786-51-5 (hard cover)
ISBN 978-981-4786-52-2 (ebook, PDF)

Typeset by Superskill Graphics Pte Ltd
Printed in Singapore by Markono Print Media Pte Ltd

Dedicated to the memory of four friends, all scholars
who had made valuable contributions to
our understanding of Southeast Asia

Cheah Boon Kheng (1939–2015),
Herbert Feith (1930–2001),
James C. Jackson (1936–1979) and
Nicholas Tarling (1931–2017)

CONTENTS

1. Introduction   1

PART I: MALAYA IN MALAYSIA

2. The Call for Malaysia   11

3. Malaya: Platform for Nation Building   36

PART II: LOCALITY IN FLUX

4. Remembering Goh Keng Swee   61

5. Before Nation: Chinese Peranakan   73

6. Singapore, Loyalty and Identity   97

7. Heritage with History   118

PART III: REFRAMING CONTEXTS

8. Reflections on Divisive Modernity   139

9. End of Empire   159

10. Family and Friends: China South and Southeast   184

Index   209

About the Author   221

Chapter 1

INTRODUCTION

When I began to put this volume together, I recalled my links with the Institute of Southeast Asian Studies (ISEAS). That reminded me of the time fifty years ago when Goh Keng Swee talked to me about establishing the institute. I was most intrigued by his foresight (see Chapter 4 on Remembering Goh Keng Swee in this volume). Other memories flooded in as I collected some of my recent writings to affirm my ISEAS connection. As a result, the book is now also a book of personal reflections and encounters about the region that the Chinese knew as Nanyang, often projected through images of Malaysia and Singapore. Behind the events after the end of World War II that shaped the new nations and settled the fates of their Chinese populations, a number of issues touching on a mixed heritage also came to mind.

In January 2016, my wife Margaret reminded me that we have lived in Singapore for twenty years. We were surprised how quickly the years had passed and noted that the period is the longest both of us have ever spent in any one place in our lives. I had spent some seventeen years growing up in Ipoh. Margaret spent the first twenty-four years of her life in Shanghai, Penang, Singapore, Cambridge, London, and back to Singapore. We then had in succession nine years in Kuala Lumpur, eighteen years in Canberra and ten years in Hong Kong. As a student, I had spent a year and a half in Nanjing, five years in Singapore and three years in London. This volume is thus also one that marks some of my changing perspectives on Singapore, Malaya and Malaysia.

I grew up as a Chinese in Malaya among millions of other Chinese in the Nanyang. Like many others, I was taught to think of China as home and my parents prepared me to return there. That day came in 1947, when the three of us moved to Nanjing, my father to teach at the school attached to his alma mater, by then renamed National Central University, and I to take the entrance examinations to seek a place at his university. I was successful and settled down to start my new life. After a very cold winter during which my father fell very ill, my mother decided that they had to return to tropical Malaya. It was a fateful decision because they would never return to China again.

I stayed on in Nanjing to learn how to be Chinese in a conflicted country that was fighting to determine what kind of modernity its people should have. By the end of 1948, the civil war came closer to us as the People's Liberation Army arrived on the northern banks of the Yangzi River. My parents were convinced that Nanjing would become a battlefield and insisted that I return to join them in Malaya. I was persuaded to do that because I was their only child.[1] Thereafter, my life changed direction. China gradually became part of my heritage, and Malaya (and places beyond) was reframed as my future.

When I first met Goh Keng Swee in London a few years later, I felt that we shared an image of that future. He could trace a different heritage from mine, but deep down it also connected at several points with China. For a couple of years, we actually belonged to the same country of Malaysia. After Singapore's separation from Malaysia in 1965, my hopes for the future were also distanced away from the Malaysian state. I returned to my studies of China and now tried to understand the China that was undergoing the fresh set of violent changes that Mao Zedong termed a Cultural Revolution. Going to the Australian National University where contemporary sources about the People's Republic were plentiful enabled me to make yet another start.[2]

This volume consists of recent writings, some looking back at the years of uncertainty after the end of World War II. Among the key changes that took place following British expansion into the Malay States at the end of the nineteenth century was the emergence of the idea of Malaya. Later, more changes followed when this Malaya was re-regrouped as Malaysia, eventually becoming Malaysia with the city-state of Singapore left out. That was a tale of twists and turns in which many Chinese played significant parts both on the peninsula and on the island. I lived through several of those turns that occurred, and vividly remember some of what followed the final stages of the story.

It so happened that two occasions provided me with opportunities to place my thoughts before an audience. The first was in Sydney at the annual meeting of the Malaysia and Singapore Society of Australia and was dedicated to a former colleague, James C. Jackson. The second was when the Malaysian Branch of the Royal Asiatic Society, together with Asia Research Institute of the NUS in Singapore, invited me to give one of its public lectures. My host was Cheah Boon Kheng and I had hoped to seek his advice to revise my text but he passed on before I could do so.

In those lectures, I did not focus on the parts played by the Chinese population or on the interests of Communist China, but both were strongly present in the Malaya-Malaysia story. Each lecture contained a touch of nostalgia for the kind of multicultural society that might have been. I must admit that the sense of regret persisted while I wrote and I realized that, despite the years since the events took place, it was still a feeling that I could not avoid.

Changes are still occurring. The part played by the Chinese Peranakan or Baba in the story may be instructive for the future, so I introduced an aspect of their story and other questions of loyalty and identity before there were modern ideas of nationhood, and also what various Chinese have done in response to the nation-building efforts around them. The locally settled were once in the frontline of Chinese adaptation to alien conditions and had developed successful strategies to deal with their predicament. Their historical experiences could serve to illustrate how Chinese communities who have settled abroad might have to handle future challenges. Thus the essay describing Baba Peranakan encounters with early ideas of nation also touches on aspects of the Chinese heritage in the Nanyang, the kind of perspective that I imagined Goh Keng Swee to have had.

That drew me to another feature of Chinese adaptability, their changing identities and the impact of that phenomenon on ideas of loyalty. What did Chinese understand about those shifts in British Singapore? How did they relate them to the cultural values and other artefacts that they or their ancestors brought from China? And what changed in Singapore when the independent city-state institutionalized the plural society it decided to uphold? Here, of course, I go back to the story of what the decision to create Greater Malaysia meant for the Chinese. In doing that, I am drawn back to contemplate the Malaya that the Chinese had got used to. That way, we can see the layers of cultural and political heritage behind the rapid developments of the past half-century.

The Chinese heritage in Singapore is now getting the attention it deserves. The fresh interest is in part because China is regaining its place in the world but the developments also come from the historical information now readily and swiftly available in numerous books and on the Internet. I suggest that this attention could deepen if there is further awareness of what their origins were like. Although what one takes from heritage does not have to adhere to the original purpose that created it, it is surprising what could continue to have relevance under conditions that have radically changed.

This led me to a different perspective, to another kind of heritage, that of divisiveness following the years of decolonization in Southeast Asia. I spoke about this in a lecture that I had delivered a few years earlier in honour of Herb Feith. Herb Feith was one of the founders of the Monash University Centre of Southeast Asian Studies and an excellent scholar of Indonesian politics. I first met him in Melbourne in July 1965. Because of the circumstances of our first meeting when we spoke about the region's ongoing conflicts, my lecture recalled that meeting and I entitled it "Divisive Modernity". Our first meeting was on the eve of the Malaysia-Singapore separation when Malaysia was not yet two years old. It was thus a meeting I keenly remember.

Herb Feith was a scholar I admired for his understanding of Sukarno's Indonesia. Talking about the divisiveness there and how it was related to the efforts to become modern led us also to wonder about the impact of China's hard communism on Indonesia's soft response. We went on to talk about the way Indonesia's leader Sukarno was determined to destroy the fledgling Malaysia and that led us to the consequences of imperial rule and the nature of empires. We even went on to talk about the religious divisions that modernity has spawned.

Two years after I gave that lecture in 2004, I found myself speaking on a happier occasion, one in honour of Nicholas Tarling's seventy-fifth birthday. At the conference organized for him, I talked about the empires we have either studied or lived through, with emphasis on their final days. The lecture was published as "Imperial Themes". Sadly, as I was revising parts of it for this volume, on 13 May 2017, Nick Tarling unexpectedly died. We had shared some experiences with empires, but how the end of the Chinese and British empires impacted on the Nanyang was a subject that we developed an ongoing interest in. China's was premodern at its core and Britain's was national and capitalism-inspired. I talked about how they cast different shadows on today's relations between a revived China and the new nations of Southeast Asia.

The last chapter, written in 2008, takes me to another recurring theme in Nanyang–China relations. I refer to the asymmetry in relationships whenever China turned its attention to the neighbours to its south. I set out to find the words and ideas in historical texts that tell us how China chose to regard these foreign rulers in smaller states. There were terms that were used consistently over the centuries and showed why the conditions for the development of what we call diplomacy and foreign affairs had not been present during all that time. The words and ideas commonly used are deeply embedded in Confucian attitudes towards those beyond their ken. They are examples of China's intangible heritage that still influence China's relations with its neighbours today.

China has now risen to economic power and global prominence and it is changing its attitudes towards smaller neighbours and those people of Chinese origins who are living overseas. In particular it appears to have different expectations of those who are recent emigrants from the Chinese mainland. How this will affect those ethnic Chinese who have fully localized will be of keen interest to all concerned. Insofar as China still appeals to the ideas and practices in past relationships, it would be necessary for countries engaged with China today to constantly and carefully update their understanding of that heritage.

Notes

1. I have completed a book of memories about my first nineteen years in Ipoh and Nanjing, entitled *Home Is Not Here*, to be published by the NUS Press in 2018.

2. My early research life (1954–61) had taken me back to ancient China's trading relations with the Nanhai (South China Sea), the politics of North China in the tenth century and the tributary relations of the early Ming dynasty. At the University of Malaya (1957–68), I taught Ming and Qing imperial history for over ten years and also aspects of comparative historical thought in Asia and Europe. During the transition from Malaya to Malaysia, my research interests turned to Malayan history and I worked with my colleagues and students to seek a local perspective I also began to focus on the tribulations of overseas Chinese communities.

   The beginnings of the Great Proletarian Cultural Revolution in Mao Zedong's China in 1965–66 reawakened my interest in contemporary China. Thus the offer of a research professorship at the Australian National University was irresistible. Not being able to gain access to any documents concerning China in an anti-communist region, I was hungry to read the excellent collections of such materials in Canberra. They absorbed my attention for several years and enabled me to write *China and the World since 1949: The impact of independence, modernity and revolution* (1977).

PART ONE

Malaya in Malaysia

Chapter 2

THE CALL FOR MALAYSIA

The call for Malaysia in 1961 was a controversial one, not least for the Chinese who had settled for generations in Singapore. In a different way, the largely local-born Chinese of the former Straits Settlements now part of Malaya — Penang and Malacca — as well as others who arrived later in the Malay States of the peninsula who had gained citizenship rights in the Federation of Malaya were also deeply affected. Many of them had hoped to see Singapore reunited with Malaya but were not sure what it meant to have two Borneo states added on when Prime Minister Tunku Abdul Rahman announced the plan to create a new federation. The proposal was greeted with scepticism in parts of peninsular Malaya as well as in the three British colonies of Singapore,

---

This chapter is a revised version of the Jackson Memorial Lecture of the Malaysia and Singapore Association of Australia given on 11 July 2012 at the Australian Association of Asian Studies Conference held at the University of West Sydney. James C. (Jim) Jackson was one of my colleagues at the University of Malaya who joined me in 1962 to produce a volume of essays to explain what the new country called Malaysia was about. In his memory, he died suddenly in 1979, I chose to recall fifty years later what that call for Malaysia meant.

Sarawak and Sabah. Elsewhere in the region, Indonesia under President Sukarno was opposed to such a federation that reached across the South China Sea to Borneo, the greater part of that island being part of Indonesia. He thus led a fierce campaign against the proposal from the start.

This was the middle of the Cold War. The new state of Malaysia was located on the maritime frontline between the forces of liberal capitalism led by Britain and the United States and the revolutionary armies that supported Soviet and Chinese communism. Not least among the concerns at the time was the reaction of the Chinese minorities in the polities that were being brought together. The question uppermost in some circles was the future of Singapore where the Chinese formed a clear majority and could democratically choose a government that was sympathetic to China and unfavourable to British and Malayan interests.

That call was over fifty years ago. I look back in wonder at what has happened since a group of my colleagues at the University of Malaya in Kuala Lumpur joined me in 1962 to put together what we knew of this Malaysia and set out to tell the world of the birth of a new country. We were not sure how viable it was but agreed that it was a step forward in the decolonization process. It was clear that knowledge of the main political units involved was very uneven, so the first thing to do was to explain what this Malaysia consisted of. We were interested in the reasons behind the British decision to package their colonies in this way before they left. We were also intrigued by Tunku Abdul Rahman's willingness to go along with a plan that included Singapore. It was well known that he was sceptical of bringing in the colony because of its large Chinese population.

It was a challenge to examine the multiple factors involved but we agreed that a survey of what was known of the past and present of this nation-to-be was necessary. We even agreed to try to have the volume ready when the federation was formed. The book, *Malaysia: A Survey,* finally appeared in 1964, a year late.[1] Its publication was delayed because the authors had to revise their drafts, including tables and graphs, when Brunei decided not to join. Then, a year after the book appeared, Singapore left the federation. The volume was now out-of-date. It was a sobering experience that taught me as editor not to be so eager to deal with contemporary subjects.

In my introduction to the book, I wrote hopefully about the country's future even though I was conscious of the long list of problems it had to face. The various states were at different stages of development. I suggested that three areas were of particular concern: the nature of the nation-state that would be created by the mixed bag of ethnic groups that were being brought together; the need to coordinate economic development for the many more varieties of rural and urban communities the country now would have; and the kind of political leaders that would emerge — men and women who were educated in diverse kinds of schools that taught in different languages in different parts of the country. Despite all that, I tried to look at the brighter side.

There were also threatening noises against the new state from outside. The most alarming was the confrontation policy launched by President Sukarno of Indonesia. He and his colleagues were completely opposed to the idea of Malaysia and set about to persuade other countries in the region and beyond to oppose the creation of the new federation. Sukarno declared that the whole thing was a neo-colonial plot that could not be tolerated while the fight against imperialism was still going on. For Southeast Asia, this war was no longer a cold one. It was becoming hotter every day with the United States replacing the French as the protector of the Vietnamese nationalist forces in the south. And Britain was America's closest ally. There were rebellions elsewhere in Southeast Asia, not least that led by the Malayan Communist Party in the Federation of Malaya as well as Singapore. In addition, a new revolutionary movement led mainly by local Chinese was growing in Sarawak. Then came the Brunei Revolt led by A.M. Azahari that was supported by the Indonesian Communists as well as sections of the Indonesian government.

My introduction identified *Konfrontasi* as a serious threat, but I clearly underestimated the range of other difficulties within the new federation that I should have anticipated.[2] This was in part due to wishful thinking and youthful optimism. Some of my colleagues were less sanguine but we agreed that our book should survey the facts about the federation and not be judgmental, so they all refrained from speculating on the complexities that Malaysian national leaders would have to face. Indeed, difficult issues remained on the table down to the last minute when the leaders could not agree whether the new nation's foundation should fall on 31 August or on 16 September 1963.

Looking back, I am fascinated by the many unexpected developments in the region and the different trajectories in the rise of East Asian economic power during the last fifty years. In particular, the tumultuous events that led to the fall of the Soviet Union and its satellite states as well as the emergence of America as the world's sole superpower have been awesome. In that larger context, the rapid rise of China and the future role of India stand out, not least because the relations between these two rising giants would focus on Southeast Asia as the bridge between the Indian and Pacific Oceans. That has opened a new page for the ten states of the Association of Southeast Asian Nations (ASEAN). If that connection is peacefully managed, the region could be the hub for nearly half the population of the world.

Great unknowns lie before us and indeed much rethinking will have to be done before the protagonists, old and new, can

hope to settle down to anything like peaceful co-existence. I shall
not try to cover the many transformations that led to the recent
developments. Instead, I shall limit myself to two observations
about what flowed from the call for Malaysia in 1961. The first
is how it ended in failure for those within, mainly Chinese and
South Asians who saw advantage in a more balanced population,
and those Malay leaders who saw Singapore as part of Tanah
Melayu and wanted the country to control the region's best
deep-water port. They had worked hard for the ideal of a single
united country. The second is that the call turned out to be an
unexpected success for others, notably those looking for ways
to shore up their economic and security interests in Asia. In
particular, these were leading powers of the day that were facing
the high tide of anti-imperialism, big business with investments in
both Malaya and Singapore that were closely associated with the
former colonial states and, not least, those who were ideological
enemies of communism. Most of them shared the interests of
the strong Anglo-American international structure that seems to
have been the only one strong enough to maintain control over
the strategic links of the global market economy.

THE FAILURE WITHIN

The first observation centres on failure and begins with the
question: In the nine Malay states and the two former Straits
Settlements of Penang and Malacca, who wanted Malaysia? These
eleven units were the component parts of what was no more
than a pre-nation, that is, a polity that was not yet a nation but
needed to build one. Such a pre-nation had only just begun in
1957 to come to grips with the demands of nationhood. When
I moved from Singapore to Kuala Lumpur in May 1959, I found
the country in the midst of the first general election of the new

Federation of Malaya. My friends took me around where the main national parties were campaigning. Four months later, the Alliance Party won 74 out of 104 seats in the federal parliament, but with only a bare majority of the popular vote, less than 52 per cent. There were only two credible opposition parties, the Pan-Malayan Islamic Party (PMIP, or Parti Islam Se-Malaysia, PAS) supported by largely Malay voters and the Malayan People's Socialist Front that was mainly supported by Chinese and Indian voters. The two together garnered more than a third of the votes.[3] Each was strong in only one or two states, but they did have different goals for the country that, at the time, were little understood, especially by the majority of the Malay people loyal to their traditional leaders.

The semblance of national unity seemed to have come from three factors. There was a broad willingness to see the British leave. There was also the perception that, unless the disparate peoples around the country were united under communal labels, each community would suffer serious loss of their rights as citizens. The third factor was stronger in some groups more than in others. It stemmed from the fear among them that any effort to depart from communal politics was likely to lead to serious class divisions. That would favour the worker-peasant majority in the new democratic system. It would encourage the communist movement and certainly threaten the interests of the aristocrats, bureaucrats and businessmen who were still in control.

Given the fact that the political issues were perplexing to most people and that the Alliance Party's election victory had been so close, there was no desire for any change to the national borders that could make the task of winning power even more difficult. With that background, it was clear that the call for Malaysia had no roots among the majority of the people. But were the leaders in various parts of the peninsula really desirous of a larger federation? A number of families who had members in both the Federation and Singapore would have preferred to see Singapore within Malaya. A large proportion of them would have been non-Malays, especially among established Peranakan families of the former Straits Settlements that had provided leaders of the Chinese community. There were some immigrants from the Malay Archipelago, from nearby Sumatra and the Riau–Lingga islands, who did not owe loyalty to any of the Malay rulers but thought Singapore should be incorporated. Many labour activists wanted closer ties with their counterparts in a united Malaya. However, there were many among the Chinese leaders of trade unions who were wary of the Anglo-Malay power structure that controlled the government in Kuala Lumpur and were less eager to change the status quo.[4]

When Tunku Abdul Rahman made the public call for Malaysia two years later, he was obviously tentative and uneasy. His United Malays National Organization (UMNO) party was not keen. Its strongest supporters in the rural areas rightly believed that the party had enough to do trying to build a nation for the Malays without adding more than a million Chinese to the national problem. But he knew that the British government was preparing to leave, and he was afraid of the left-wing opposition that was in sympathy with the communist rebellion. Together with his most trusted colleagues, he weighed the alternatives and concluded that the only thing better than a merger with Singapore was to extend the Federation and accept the British gift of the three north Bornean states of Sarawak, Brunei and Sabah. Thus, it was left to only a few men to decide whether or not to make the Malaysia call. In Singapore, the number of men involved in responding to the call was just as few. Led by Lee Kuan Yew's People's Action Party (PAP), they thought that the alternative to merger was an unstable colony that would be increasingly dominated by the left wing. While the Left was keen to join the PAP in seeking independence for Singapore, the British and Malayan leaders would not agree to that if it meant allowing the Left to win power.[5]

The Malaysia call was, therefore, a top-down nation-building exercise that was calibrated and rationalized. It was not an offspring of any kind of nationalism and carried little passion or commitment. It was at best the brainchild of forward planning and at worst an abstract ideal — either could be used by political leaders to justify defensive actions against their political enemies. What then were the elite groups planning for? There was no consensus. Among the nationalist Malay leaders who accepted the plan, they had the advantage of constitutional legitimacy, and there was near unanimity among them against any kind of leftist republicanism. If the call for Malaysia could lead them to greater security for the communal power they commanded, it was right that they should go ahead.

As for the Chinese and Indians, after a decade of indecision about where they really belonged, many were by 1957 ready to identify with Malaya. For them, adding a few more states to the federation of Malaya and a slight change in the country's name was not that serious a matter. For them to identify with the new Malaysia was no more an uphill struggle than what they had already been through since the end of World War II. Indeed, in many respects, there was by 1961 an acceptable compromise settlement and a clear direction for the country to grow. Therefore, those who cared for the future of their chosen new home felt that they could live with the enlargements that their leaders agreed to.

What of the peoples of northern Borneo? What did they know about Malaya and Singapore? They had every reason to be sceptical. Their leaders hoped ultimately to gain independence for their respective states and were unprepared for the Malaysia call. They were, in any case, given very little time to organize themselves to deal with the question. Only the Sultan of Brunei had the choice to decide for himself and he eventually chose to stay out. The British, once they had the leaders of Malaya and Singapore on their side, moved swiftly and used all the credit they still had in Sarawak and Sabah to bring their protégés to the Malaysia table. The deed was done before anyone in both territories could sort out what had already been agreed to by the major players. The Malaysia call required urgent response, and the British got what they wanted in quick time and with the minimum fuss.

In short, the call for Malaysia mattered little in the eyes of most people. They assumed that their leaders knew what they were doing and were ready to make the most of what ensued. The only success that was important was their economic well-being and a minimum sense of security. What kind of nation would come of it, whether the federation would succeed or fail, was not of grave concern as long as the interests of each community seemed to be assured.

Although the issue was more complicated for the people of Singapore, what they focused on was how autonomous Singapore could remain under their own strong leadership. Also, many could already see how British interventions with support from Malaya had actually helped strengthen the Singapore leadership. If their demand for autonomy in the new Malaysia were unacceptable to central leaders in Kuala Lumpur and, at the same time, unsatisfactory for the majority in the city-state, then Singapore in Malaysia would be a grave problem rather than the solution that the elites in both territories desired.

The Singapore problem surfaced almost immediately after Malaysia Day in 1963. I observed this from my office on the campus of the University of Malaya in Kuala Lumpur and followed the negotiations as best I could. They continued for months as Singapore held out for the safest deal they could obtain from a reluctant federal leadership.[6] By early May 1965, while I was away at the Australian National University, the tensions had mounted beyond help. On my last day in Canberra, on 9 August, it was over. I heard the news when I was lunching with Malaysia desk officers of the Australian Ministry of External Affairs. They were as surprised as I was when they were urgently called back to their office.

With Singapore out, the call for Malaysia had obviously failed. Singapore was left to find its own path to nationhood. The thirteen states of the new Malaysian federation treaded carefully to find a new spirit to take the country forward. Its political leaders struggled to decide whether to be even more communal-oriented or to consider some non-communal approaches to the country's future. I was drawn to support my friends who sought a middle way between the Malay constitutional monarchy under which the government functioned or the plural society model that came to serve as the basis for Singapore's nation-building efforts. Whatever hopes remained of a non-communal polity that many people had wanted were set aside four years later in 1969. This came after an election in which the ruling coalition of communal parties was shocked by unexpected defeats at the polls. The results troubled dissident groups among the Malay nationalists and led to the tragic riots of Kuala Lumpur that broke out on 13 May 1969. With the Emergency framework that was installed to deal with the riots, communal-centred politics regained ascendency, with the UMNO achieving unchallenged control over national affairs for decades.[7]

There was a parallel failure for the ideal of Malaysian Malaysia. This was one that stressed the equality of all citizens of the future federation, no matter what their ethnic origins or communal identities. It was an ideal that Singapore leaders had advocated as the goal of the new federation, and it had the support of many of their Sarawak and Sabah partners although it was not part of any blueprint that all parties had agreed on before the Malaysia call was answered. The British, and those they had educated both locally and in the United Kingdom, probably had some understanding that such a development was desirable and possible, but it was Singapore that made the principle explicit in the political negotiations and campaigns that followed. Once stated baldly and with fervour, alarm bells began to ring in KL. The debates that followed in parliament and during the campaigns leading to the elections of 1964 publicly and forcefully underlined the different expectations that various groups had had when the Malaysia call was first made.

What the Tunku and his cabinet were afraid of was starkly brought into the open. Malaysian Malaysia was formulated because the leaders in Singapore realized that the longer term agenda in KL for a larger Malay nation-state was not what they wanted. They brought that into the open when they sensed that it was also not what most non-Malays, especially the Chinese community, in the fourteen territories had in mind for themselves and their descendants. By this exposure, the presumption of a shared goal among the leaders who negotiated the initial agreements was shown to have been wrong. The arguments the British used to persuade reluctant or sceptical leaders were expedient. They were based on strategic realities like the danger of Southeast Asia falling into leftist or communist hands and, on the global stage, the balance of power between the forces of open markets and those of class war. If they had doubts about how the future nation-state of Malaysia might develop, they thought they could leave that to be worked out later through trust, compromise and political engineering. Ideally, as the British saw it, this could be done with their help and protection, with the assistance of Commonwealth partners like Australia and New Zealand.

But time was the enemy. The British wanted to move much more quickly than the others. The tight timetable added to the tensions as the leaders in each state scrambled to calculate their respective interests and put their strongest case on the table. When deep concerns could not be satisfied, much was left for further discussion in the hope that more goodwill will surface as the leaders began to work together in the new country. There was, especially among the English-educated, the possibility that their brand of shared values, combined with political skills acquired from their British education, could pull them through. There were also others who were aroused by the intense debates and became increasingly suspicious of the hasty deal. These included those in every state who were educated in Chinese and Malay schools and were not educated by the British, not least among those in Singapore, Sarawak and Sabah. Although these sceptics could not stop what was about to happen, they were ready to challenge its progress in any way they could.

In this context, the Malaysian Malaysia slogan devised by Singapore polarized popular opinion. Some of the slogan's supporters were genuine believers and had the sympathy of their British and ANZAC (Australia and New Zealand Army Corps) friends, as well as those Americans who were engaged elsewhere in nation building. But it flew in the face of what the leaders in KL wanted and confirmed their doubts about including Singapore in the first place. The result was a confrontation of goals that ended in Singapore's departure. Thus the call for Malaysia failed on both counts. It did not bring Singapore into the family and, after its separation, also eliminated from the remaining thirteen states the possibility of the Malaysian Malaysia ideal that it had urged on the country.

Singapore gained its independence, and that new beginning was the unexpected product of the failed Malaysia call. Sarawak and Sabah, left to sort out their future in Malaysia, did not get what they wanted but were momentous gains for the leaders of the Federation of Malaya. The thirteen states that remained had to start afresh with its peoples wondering how to find a new sense of direction. Many people were tempted by the lure of communal protectionism or, if that was not possible, to seek the safety of local identities. For example, in relatively homogeneous Kelantan, its people looked to their own needs; while in Penang where there were a rich variety of cultures and histories, the people looked more outwards. Singapore eventually overcame the problems brought out by separation. Its success today is now measured in terms of its high standards of living, its efficiency and productivity, and the wide respect it has gained for incorruptibility.

Malaysia recovered from the surgery in 1965 and was eventually able to bring its political heterogeneity under control. It restructured the Malay power base to safeguard the community's security so that even the then large Chinese minority of some 30 per cent of the population would have to be content with less political space than before. But the accommodations, although challenged several times, did work out over the decades and are still broadly in place. The complex demographics of each state in the federation offer difficulties that the central power could not simply put aside. New permutations of power sharing have to be managed and, after over fifty years, this task continues to engage the country's political leaders.[8] However, there remain inadequacies in the system of effective checks and balances, and many in the country feel that the enormous potential of the country has been unfulfilled.

THE SUCCESS OUTSIDE

Looking at the Malaysia call from the outside, however, the results seem to be significantly different. I have already mentioned that, almost immediately, the British had got what they wanted. In northern Borneo, they were freed from further responsibility in Sarawak and Sabah while retaining the goodwill of the Sultanate of Brunei. In West Malaysia, they lost some credibility with the leaders but nevertheless held on to most of their economic interests for a while longer. And, although thwarted in keeping Singapore within Malaysia, they found that the PAP leadership of the independent state could be depended on to fight side by side with them against the radical anti-colonialists whom they saw as soft on communism. Although the Malaysia that the British and the PAP leaders had called for did not proceed as expected, what resulted produced similar results in the end. Of course, having two entities instead of a single united Malaysia did require that greater efforts had to be made to ensure that the new city-state of Singapore could grow up as a reliable partner in the region's affairs. For that, the keen support of allies in the Cold War was invaluable.

Of particular interest was the perspective of the United States. The study by Joey Long has established how relieved the Americans were that the heart of Southeast Asia was becoming "safe for decolonization". This was vital because the war in Vietnam had become more deadly every day. The Cold War was moving southwards. All the dominoes needed propping up. The earlier American efforts to shore up their defences, through organizations like the Southeast Asia Treaty Organization (SEATO), were not getting anywhere. The various attempts to destabilize Sukarno's Indonesia had also gone awry. Their allies in Thailand and the Philippines were doing somewhat better than they had done in the 1950s, but the British pillars of Malaysia and Singapore in between those two were crucial to American plans to keep communism from spreading in Southeast Asia.[9] They were delighted that Soviet and Chinese powers could now be kept out of this key part of their global maritime network.

The years 1961–63 also coincided with a bit of a watershed in Asian affairs. In the east, that was the beginning of Japan's spectacular economic recovery after the war. Its export-oriented model was so attractive that a new momentum of development came to inspire South Korea, Taiwan, Hong Kong and Singapore to become the Asian Tigers of the next two decades. They were also the years when the alternative vision against Cold War ideologies, the neutralism that sprang from the Bandung Conference a few years earlier in 1955, was to run aground. That neutralist alternative had been controversial and directionless for years. But between 1959 and 1962, including the years of the Malaysia call, it had reached a turning point.[10] That came from the fallout in Sino-Indian relations that ended in 1962 with the disastrous war on their Himalayan borders. As a result, India paid little attention to the Malaysia call and its aftermath. Indeed, India seemed to have switched off altogether for decades where maritime Southeast Asia was concerned. Their concerns with Pakistan, Kashmir and related problems in their northwest induced its leaders to develop closer relations with the Soviet Union instead.

The Malaysia call did concern the communist leaders in China, largely because of their commitments to its fraternal parties in the Malay world. They were anxious for their comrades in the Malayan jungle and encouraged others, including the Chinese communities, to revolt in Sarawak. But, most of all, they looked to the Parti Kommunis Indonesia (PKI) to gain further ground in Java and also supported President Sukarno in his *Konfrontasi* campaigns against Malaysia. Unfortunately for them, the perception that the Chinese Communist Party (CCP) sought local Chinese support, and was mainly interested to help these local Chinese, undermined their influence in the region.[11] On the one hand, the Chinese background of left-wing oppositions in Singapore and Malaysia handicapped their activities among those who were not Chinese. On the other, their ideology was seen as a barrier to economic enterprise among those Chinese who merely wanted to continue doing business and secure their livelihoods in their adopted countries.

Furthermore, the Malaysia call years also coincided with the climax of China's disastrous Great Leap Forward (1960–62) and the power struggle that followed within the CCP. It led Mao Zedong to spend years preparing to fight back against those of his party colleagues who had criticized his policies and tried to sideline him. Among the consequences of that struggle were further estrangement from the Soviet Union, drastic and painful efforts to recover from widespread famines, and disillusionment among Chinese communities overseas about China's economic performance.

There were many other surprising developments around Asia but, in the end, it was an event much closer to Malaysia and Singapore that totally astonished us. I refer to the Gestapu coup or September 30 Movement in Jakarta that was as unexpected as Singapore's nationhood. Within weeks of Singapore's separation from Malaysia, the murderous events that led to the downfall of Sukarno and his left-wing supporters had begun.[12] The two newly established states were relieved to watch the *Konfrontasi* campaign wind down and welcomed the new Indonesia under President Suharto.

Were Malaysia and Singapore simply lucky that Sukarno was removed from power and his *Konfrontasi* plans failed? If Sukarno had pressed on with his opposition for several more years, how would Singapore have coped? Could the leaders in KL fight on in northern Borneo if the British continued to draw their troops home? Would ANZAC forces be ready to fill the gap? How would the Americans have responded? If Sukarno had continued to move towards socialism with the PKI by his side, there would have been other serious challenges to the status quo all over the archipelago. That would have given the forces of revolution many advantages in the Cold War struggle.

We might also ask a different kind of question. Did the call for Malaysia contribute to the sudden turn of events in Sukarno's Indonesia? I think it could have done, but not directly. The strategic planning by the British that enabled a smooth decolonization along Indonesia's Bornean borders had undermined the political Left in Singapore. Those plans also secured a stronger Anglo-American post-colonial arrangement for what remained of the new Federation of Malaysia. Taken together, this was a major victory for the anti-communists. As a result, it could have triggered one of two actions. One was to encourage Leftist groups in Indonesia to move prematurely and launch the putsch to try to take control of the military, hence the abortive Gestapu coup attempt. The other was to give greater confidence to Sukarno's more conservative enemies within the military and his government to take retaliatory action so effectively.

Another longer term consequence of the call for Malaysia deserves closer attention. Those who wanted Singapore to be merged into the enlarged Malaysia to become one country may have failed, but those who led the anti-communist forces in the Archipelago were able to strengthen the regional security organization they wanted. This led in 1967 to the creation of the Association of Southeast Asian Nations (ASEAN), a new regional organization that was aligned to the West. No one could have predicted that, thirty years later when Cambodia finally joined it in 1999, this organization would expand to cover all ten countries of Southeast Asia, including three Communist states and a Myanmar that had been strenuously neutralist. A decade later, this organization has moved further ahead and promises to serve as a valuable platform for international relations in an awakened Asia.[13]

Fifty years after the Malaysia call, there are at least two other dimensions of change that are worth noting. First, two new nation-states have been established as the result of the failure of the Malaysia call. As a result of separation, both countries were economically weaker and more dependent on British and Commonwealth help than they would have been had they been one country. Both would have to develop in the world of multinational markets and transnational identities. Singapore, being small and nimble and already an established regional port, was better positioned to respond to global economic changes. Where Malaysia was concerned, nation building was much more complex, given the delicate relationships between the peninsula states and the two larger states of East Malaysia. Fortunately, both those states added to Malaysia's already rich natural and human resources. The potential for future development was much greater than that for Singapore.

Even more interesting, the separation of Singapore meant that there were two models of the modern nation-state next to one another, both of which to be found within the British Commonwealth. The basic model, that in Britain and most of the European states created since the nineteenth century, was conceived on the basis that native peoples shared the same language, religion and history and constituted the privileged citizens, the core of the nation. From time to time, they were prepared, with varying degrees of enthusiasm, to accept small numbers of immigrant peoples as future fellow citizens. The alternative model was that developed in the New World of the Americas, notably in the United States after the Thirteen Colonies gained their independence. By the twentieth century, this was accepted model for other former British colonies like Australia, New Zealand and Canada where political leaders were influenced by the example of America as a country of immigrant origin. Having taken land from indigenous peoples, the early colonists had shaped their new nations on the foundation of serial migrations and become immigrant states open to ideas of multiculturalism.

The Malay leaders in Malaysia leant towards the first model although the mix of Malay sultanates, former colonies and the two states of Sarawak and Sabah with their unique histories did not resemble the United Kingdom or any of the other European nation-states in any way. On the other hand, Singapore, as a former colony based on immigrant plural societies, was inclined to look at the newer immigrant-state model, although its history was quite different if not unique. In trying to redefine what was first spelt out in the Malaysian Malaysia ideal, Singapore's leaders looked to some of the principles of nationhood that were evolved in the American and Australasian framework. The Malaysia Call had invited an extraordinary mix of states with a variety of demographics to come together. This had the potential to make different kinds of states out of communities with a multiplicity of languages, religions and histories. What was challenging, no matter how unrealistic it might have seemed to many, was the possibility of several major Asian traditions being shaped over time to produce one distinct Malaysian or Singapore culture.

Although the two new countries set out to follow different national models, Malaysia did not have the preconditions to become a "native" country like Britain, and Singapore did not evolve from "immigrant" colonies like the states of Australia.

Therefore, each of the two new countries had the opportunity to develop its own distinct kind of multicultural state. In Malaysia's case, it would develop from the base of Malay-*bumiputera* (sons of the soil) nationalism enclosed by the idea of Malay-Chinese-Indian partnership. With Singapore, however, the new nation would be centred on a variety of small Chinese, Malay and Indian immigrant communities, each committed to working together to ensure the new country's economic growth and cultural autonomy. Fifty years on, both countries are closer to defining what each wants. But the world is changing rapidly. Various kinds of Western "soft power" as well as the revival of other traditions drawing on Indian, Chinese and Islamic cultures have become embedded in the two countries. Together with other countries in the region that are evolving various Asian perspectives on modernity, Malaysia and Singapore, with five decades of interactions between them, seem capable of producing distinctive kinds of nationhood.[14]

The second dimension of change is the product of some positive but unintended consequences. As briefly outlined earlier, there have been fifty very eventful years for the region as a whole and some unintended consequences of the Malaysia call can be seen as follows. These began in the late 1960s with the impending American defeat in Vietnam. Had the archipelago defence line of Malaysia-Singapore not held and the Sukarno government not replaced, it could have led to greater failures for the anti-communist cause. But the Vietnam disaster for the Americans brought about realignments that were unintended. The Vietnamese had turned to the Soviet Union for help and the Chinese were given a marginal role although the war was close to its borders. This was one of the straws that broke the back of the Sino-Soviet alliance. It meant that both China and the United States were, at the same time though in different ways, being defeated in Southeast Asia. That helped to open the door for the two countries to re-examine their relationship.[15] The Kissinger trip to Beijing to see Zhou Enlai in 1971 was the turning point. It enabled President Nixon to visit Mao Zedong the next year to mark a total change of policy direction. Their fruitful meetings upended the Cold War central balance that had provided some degree of global security for decades.

In Southeast Asia, the end of Sino-Indonesian friendship following the fall of Sukarno had opened up another set of alignments. The entry of the People's Republic as the only China in the United Nations in November 1971, followed by the Nixon visit, opened the way for Malaysia to establish formal diplomatic ties in 1975. In the context of the new Malaysian vision after 13 May 1969, this was a brilliant move on the part of Prime Minister Tun Razak. It underlined the multicultural nature of the country in which its large Chinese ethnic minority had a legitimate political place. It gave that community a sense of acceptance as loyal citizens who had an important role in building friendly relations with the PRC. In contrast, Singapore with its Chinese majority thought it had to be more cautious. Although it already had close commercial relations with China, it needed to assure its neighbours that its relationship would never be at the expense of good neighbourly relations in the region. This was particularly true of its need for the trust and friendship of President Suharto's Indonesia. As a result, Singapore delayed its formal recognition of China until Sino-Indonesian diplomatic relations was restored in 1990. Thus it was not until fifteen years after Malaysia that Singapore felt able to establish official diplomatic relations with China.

This can be seen as an unintended consequence of the failure of the call for Malaysia. I am struck by the relative ease by which Malaysia confidently established relations with the PRC in 1975. It leads me to ask, what would Sino-Malaysia relations have been like if Singapore had remained a constituent part of Malaysia? Looking back, it would seem that, by becoming two separate states, there developed two ways for each of them to engage China and Indonesia, the two most important countries for them both. We can look at three stages in the relationships.

For the first period, 1965–75, there was no question of any formal relationship with China by either country; the contrast was in their respective relations with Indonesia. Singapore's relations started badly when Singapore executed the two Indonesian marines whose bombs killed and wounded many Singaporeans. Eventually, the leaders of Indonesia and Singapore did succeed in building a close relationship that also determined how cautiously Singapore had to deal with any relationship with China as long as Sino-Indonesian relations were frozen. Malaysia was different. The relief it felt when Sukarno was removed was palpable. Not surprising, normal relations prevailed.

Everything became more different in the second period, 1975–90. Malaysia proceeded to recognize the PRC in 1975. This was politically astute in every way. It satisfied the ethnic Chinese partners in the Alliance Party and opened up commercial relations that became increasingly profitable for Malaysian companies, especially after Deng Xiaoping's economic reforms began three years later. Singapore held back diplomatically but engaged China by other means and was no less successful after Deng Xiaoping's visit to Southeast Asia in November 1978. Significantly, the lack of formal relations was no barrier at all. Where Indonesia was concerned, Singapore knew it had to make greater efforts and was duly rewarded with increasingly warm ties, especially between the two country's leaders.

For the third period since 1990, Singapore established diplomatic relations with the PRC, following the resumption of formal links between China and Indonesia. All is now publicly normal. But differences between Malaysia and Singapore where China is concerned remain remarkable. Singapore's relations are largely commercial and administrative, with careful arrangements for the more sensitive areas of political and cultural ties. Malaysia seems more relaxed, even in delicate matters pertaining to religion and the recognition of Chinese educational qualifications. The subject deserves more careful study. It is enough here to point out that the enhanced freedom of action possible for the two separate countries has greatly benefited both Malaysia and Singapore. For me, it is hardly possible to imagine what the relationships with Indonesia and China would have been like had Singapore remained in Malaysia. It seems appropriate to describe this freedom that has contributed to excellent relations between the PRC and both Malaysia and Singapore as being one of the positive unintended consequence of the bitter separation in 1965.

I have outlined the reasons why the call for Malaysia may be considered a small failure when compared with the successes that followed for most of the elites in both countries and the governments that they led. The failure was even smaller when we consider the much bigger successes for the major national protagonists of the region, not to say the winners in the global Cold War.

Notes

1. *Malaysia: A survey*, edited by Wang Gungwu (New York and London: Praeger and Pall Mall Press, 1964).
2. It was not until years later when I read the excellent study by Jamie Mackie that I understood the full complexities of the *Konfrontasi* campaign against Malaysia; J.A.C. Mackie, *Konfrontasi: The Indonesia-Malaysia dispute, 1963–1966* (Kuala Lumpur & New York: Australian Institute of International Affairs and Oxford University Press, 1974).

3. T.E. Smith, "The Malaya elections of 1959", *Pacific Affairs* 33, no. 1 (1960): 38–47.

4. Lee Ting Hui, *The open united front: The communist struggle in Singapore, 1954–1966* (Singapore: South Seas Society, 1996).

5. The opening chapters of Albert Lau's *A moment of anguish: Singapore in Malaysia and the politics of disengagement* (Singapore: Times Academic Press, 1998).

6. Tan Tai Yong, *Creating "Greater Malaysia": Decolonisation and the politics of merger* (Singapore: Institute of Southeast Asian Studies, 2008).

7. Raj K. Vasil, *Ethnic politics in Malaysia* (New Delhi: Radiant Publishers, 1980).

8. Abdul Rahman Haji Ismail and Azmi Arifin, eds., *Sejarah Malaysia: Wacana Kedaulatan Bangsa, Kenegaraan dan Kemerdekaan* (Pulau Pinang: Penerbit Universiti Sains Malaysia, 2016); Johan Saravanamuttu, *Power Sharing in a Divided Nation: Mediated Communalism and New Politics in Six Decades of Malaysia's Elections* (Singapore: ISEAS – Yusof Ishak Institute, 2016).

9. Joey Long Shi Ruey, *Safe for decolonization: The Eisenhower administration, Britain, and Singapore* (Kent, Ohio: Kent State University Press, 2011); John Subritzky, *Confronting Sukarno: British, American, Australian and New Zealand diplomacy in the Malaysian-Indonesian confrontation, 1961–5* (New York: St. Martin's Press, 1999): Gareth Porter, *Perils of dominance: Imbalance of power and the road to war in Vietnam* (Berkeley: University of California Press, 2005).

10. Tan See Seng and Amitav Acharya, eds., *Bandung revisited: The legacy of the 1955 Asian-African Conference for international order* (Singapore: NUS Press, 2008).

11. Chin Peng, *My side of history* (Singapore: Media Masters, 2003); 余柱业 (Eu Chooi Ip), 《浪尖逐梦: 余柱业口述历史档案》 [Eu Chooi Yip's Oral History Memoirs]. 陈剑主编 (Petaling Jaya: 策略资讯研究中心, Strategic Information and Research Development Centre, 2006); 方壮璧, 《方壮璧回忆录》 [Fong Chong Pik: the Memoirs of a Malayan Communist Revolutionary] (Petaling Jaya: 策略资讯研究中心, 2006).

12. Putu Oka Sukanta, ed. *Breaking the silence: Survivors speak about 1965–66 violence in Indonesia*, translated by Jennifer Lindsay (Clayton: Monash University Publishing, 2014); Douglas Kammen and Katherine McGregor, eds., *The contours of mass violence in Indonesia, 1965–1968* (Singapore: NUS Press, 2012). Compare the versions on the coup by Benedict Anderson and Ruth McVey, *A preliminary analysis of the October 1, 1965, coup in Indonesia* (Ithaca, NY: Modern Indonesia Project, Cornell University, 1971) and Nugroho Notosusanto and Ismail Saleh, *The coup attempt of the "September 30 Movement" in Indonesia* (Jakarta: Pembinang Masa, 1968).

13. Kishore Mahbubani and Jeffrey Sng, *The ASEAN Miracle: A catalyst for peace* (Singapore: NUS Press, 2017).

14. I have described them as nation-building work-in-progress, in "What if the nation-state is no longer the key organizational unit of the international community?", *Singapore Perspectives, 2017: What If?*, edited by Gillian Koh and Debbie Soon (Singapore: Institute of Policy Studies and World Scientific Publishing Co., 2018), pp. 19–30.

15. Henry Kissinger, *Ending the Vietnam War: A personal history of America's involvement in and extrication from the Vietnam War* (New York: Simon & Schuster, 2003); Yukinori Komine, *Secrecy in US foreign policy: Nixon, Kissinger and the rapprochement with China* (Aldershot, UK; Burlington: Ashgate, 2008).

Chapter 3

MALAYA
Platform for Nation Building

The transition from Malaya as a state to the new federation of
Malaysia has not been easy to explain. Whether any part of
what Malaya stood for still guides its successor state is also hard
to determine. There have frequently been complaints about the
different names for the lands of the Malays and how difficult
it is to distinguish between the use of the two words, Malaya
and Malaysia. They are the two names that still cause confusion
from time to time. It is important to distinguish between the
two because Malaysia is now well established as an established
country while Malaya has become a historical name. Nevertheless,
Malaya has an interesting lineage and served for fifteen years as

This chapter is a revised version of the MBRAS (Malaysian Branch of the Royal
Asiatic Society) Lecture given on 12 October 2013. The original title was "Malaya
and New Paths to Nationhood" and it was organized together with the Asia
Research Institute of the National University of Singapore. Cheah Boon Kheng
(1939–2015), one of the finest historians of contemporary Malaya, gave me the
honour of chairing the meeting. This lecture is included here in his remembrance.

the nation-to-be. What I shall explore here is how that name once evoked a set of ideas and institutions that came to serve as the foundations of a new nation-state. Now that the name has been put aside, the interesting question is whether Malaya's heritage of ideas and institutions has survived in the two nations that emerged from it that were once expected to be part of a single nation.

Malaya began as "British Malaya". The Malay peoples never liked that and preferred to use Tanah Melayu (Malay Land). The Chinese, on the other hand, readily translated the English name into "Malaya belonging to England" (英属马来亚). Later, "British" was removed when the Malayan Union was established, but so also was the colony that was its main port, Singapore. When the Federation of Malaya replaced the Union, the Malays kept the name Tanah Melayu and used Persekutuan for Federation.[1] The Chinese called the Union 马来亚合邦 and then changed that to 联邦 (Federation) in 1948 but kept Malaya in the country's name.

This Malaya fought the communist threat, using a formula for multi-communal politics and eventually gained independence from British rule in 1957. Six years later, the British offer of the nearby states they controlled — Brunei, Sarawak and Sabah — to create a new Malaysia federation was announced and actually came to pass in 1963. It did not last. Singapore left two years later and the Malaysia plan ended up by becoming two independent states. Neither used the name of Malaya again.

What's in a name? I have asked from time to time if anything was left of Malaya as a nation-building platform. I had even wondered if that Malaya disappeared altogether or if what happened was much more than a mere name change. And, if what Malaya stood for has not gone away altogether, what parts of that Malaya have survived? Others may have asked similar questions. The answers would depend on where you are sitting.

At least, I expect they would be different from the perspective of Kuala Lumpur and of Singapore. I lived in Malaya before and after 1948, in Malaya from 1959 to 1963 and in Malaysia from 1963 to 1968. After some thirty years away, I came to Singapore in 1996 and have been living here since. When the city-state celebrated its half-century of independence in 2015, I joined my friends in the festivities. That event reminded me of some old question, whether separating from Malaysia was Singapore's only way forward. But, more to the point, I wondered if the two states still operate within the frame that Malaya had once provided. Thinking about that led me to recollect the evolution of Malaya and also consider if that Malaya had a place in the separate paths taken by the two states after 1965.

SINGAPORE IN MALAYA

Singapore was part of a multiple-state colonial entity called British Malaya since at least the beginning of the twentieth century. It was left out of the Malayan Union when that was conceived in London during World War II. After a brief interlude, 1946–48, the Federation of Malaya replaced the Union. The new protectorate consisted of nine Malay sultanates and two of the Straits Settlements less Singapore. In 1957, these became the independent Federation of Malaya, leaving Singapore still a colony. In 1961, the British persuaded Prime Minister Tunku Abdul Rahman that a larger federation of Malaysia could include Singapore as well as the states in northern Borneo. With remarkable energy, the British persuaded all parties to agree that this Greater Malaysia would be the best outcome for all concerned when Britain departs as an imperial power. That federation was proclaimed in 1963. Less than two years later, Singapore was separated, an event greeted with relief by some, with celebratory fireworks by others, and with regrets among the rest. Although very few people were active participants in this drama, no one was unaffected by the result.

There are numerous books that chart the changes in each country, and particular attention has been given to the governance in the countries and the impact on people's lives. Here I shall focus on the British idea of Malaya as a platform for state building and its fate with or without Singapore. I begin with the historical artefact, the imaginary, of British Malaya. When I was growing up in the state of Perak, one of the four Federated Malay States (FMS) under British protection, it was normal to write about Malaya in English and Chinese. During the Japanese occupation (1942–45), the peninsular mainland was Ma-rai-ee, with Singapore separately named as Syonan-to.[2] As far as I know, this was the only place-name that was changed to a Japanese name after they took control in Southeast Asia which suggests that the Japanese meant to retain Singapore as their colony. The idea that Singapore was separate, or should be separated, from the rest of Malaya probably began with that change.

When the British returned three years later, they introduced the name of Malayan Union. This was during my last year in school in 1946. Soon after, I went to university in China. When I returned at the end of 1948, the Union had been renamed the Federation of Malaya. I qualified to be a Federal Citizen[3] and resumed my studies in the new University of Malaya. My fellow students saw decolonization as inevitable and noted how the process was speeded up around us. We expected the country to become an independent multicultural country before long. In anticipation, we prepared ourselves to be Malayans.[4]

Those were exhilarating and uncertain times. We knew that an independent new country would face serious challenges from both communists and communalists. It was obvious that a decisive struggle among the contending parties would come sooner rather than later. Most of the students were from the Federation (the nine Malay states, Penang and Malacca), with less than a third from Singapore, but many shared the hope that we would one day be united in a country called Malaya. We were conscious that the university was modelled on British and other Commonwealth universities, but were confident that Malaya would develop its own local character when the time came.

Our attention was focused on the political leadership that was engaged in the war against the Malayan Communist Party under Chin Peng while seeking independence from the British. Two political clubs were established on campus, and both were opposed to any communalist approach towards national politics. One supported socialist views that the anti-colonialists favoured. The other was critical of left-wing politics. It was, nevertheless, taken for granted that a Malayan nation was what will be created, even though there was little agreement as to what such a nation would be like.[5]

The demographic imbalance on campus was obvious. Malay students formed a small minority of the student body. Their leaders chose to be active off campus where the Malay cause was central to their future. Looking back, Malay concerns about the Malaya that the British and the English-educated were imagining were taken too lightly. Similarly, another kind of alienation was also taking place. That involved the thousands of Chinese students graduating from the Chinese schools who, following the Communist victory in China, were deprived of the higher education for which they were qualified. From the point of view of those Malay and Chinese students, the idea that the English-educated and British-trained leadership would inherit the colonial state and use it to shape the country that they wanted was unpalatable.[6]

In fact, tensions within the society had been growing since the end of the war. They became even more serious when the

Malayan Union was abandoned in 1948 after being in existence for less than two years. During all that time, the name of Malaya that non-Malays were using freely continued to be called Tanah Melayu among Malays. Even when the name was kept as the official name of the new federation, the country remained Tanah Melayu in the eyes of more than half the country's population.

BRITISH MALAYA

Today, most people see Malaya as an outdated concept best left to historians. I shall argue here that it would be wrong to dismiss it altogether. Following the separation of Singapore from Malaysia, the two countries took different roads towards their future: the city-state path and the nation-state path. But that did not mean that the two paths headed in totally different directions. The choices each had made may have departed in some ways from the Malaya model, but it should not be assumed that nothing of that Malaya remained. I shall show that it is useful to recall how Malaya evolved and what Malaya was expected to stand for.

British Malaya began as shorthand for the colony and the Malay states during the first decades of the twentieth century. Books by senior British officials like Hugh Clifford and Frank Swettenham popularized the name. By the 1920s, the name was widely used, notably the *Illustrated Guide to British Malaya* at the British Empire Exhibition in 1924. British control was well understood and taken for granted, and sometimes the word "British" was omitted, for example, in Richard Winstedt's *Malaya: The Straits Settlements and the Federated and Unfederated Malay States.*[7] Another was when the name of the Straits Branch of the Royal Asiatic Society was changed in 1923 to the Malayan Branch. Thereafter Malaya was generally accepted by the outside world. When the South Seas (Nanyang) Communist Party in Singapore was dissolved in 1930, it was replaced by one named the *Malayan Communist Party*. The party proclaimed that it represented the working classes of the Straits Settlements and all the states on the Malay Peninsula.[8] Chinese books that described the Malay States as Malaiya 马来亚 soon used the name to include the Straits Settlements (海峡殖民地) as well. It is hard to believe that they all saw Malaya through the same lens.

The British focused on the polities that came under their control after the 1870s — the four Malay sultanates that were added to the Straits Settlements colony. The four were rich in resources, but disorderly and thinly populated. It was time for the trade and industry revolution that had engulfed the world and created the port cities of Penang and Singapore to be extended further into the jungles on the Malay Peninsula. More mines and plantations offered profits and revenues. With a law-based administration, new capital and intakes of foreign labour, economic development could proceed. The input of British management drawn from the adjacent colony was expected to help produce a new state on Malay land.

There were three major themes in the efforts to realize this idea of a modern Malaya. The first was that of capital and labour. Capital came from Britain, British India and other parts of the Empire, and the Chinese, Arab and other merchant communities in the region. Labour was introduced mostly from China and British India but also from neighbouring Sumatra and Java. When the workers settled, they added considerable numbers to the population and laid the foundations of a plural society.

As capital accumulated and the workforce grew, administrative needs became greater. This led to the second theme of sound management. The mix of direct colonial rule and indirect control of Malay polities required a great range of skills. There were growing demands for infrastructure investment, for law and order, for ensuring peaceful communal relations, for health care and literacy and a host of other problems that were thrown up as capital and labour expanded further inland. Additional changes in indirect rule followed when more Malay states came into the British orbit, notably the four states in the north, Kedah and Perlis, Kelantan and Trengganu, that the British shifted out of the Thai tributary system early in the twentieth century. Then there was the question of the sovereignty of the Malay state of Johor and its special relationship with Singapore. The untidiness became unbearable. Where do these five states fit into the Malaya the British had identified? The clumsy use of Unfederated Malay States was both baffling and laughable.

Puzzling over such nomenclature led to fresh thinking about the third theme, that of centralization. The drive began in the 1920s towards stronger direction from Singapore and Kuala Lumpur, towards greater control of people and property whether directly or in the name of Malay sultans.[9] Legitimizing the use of power became increasingly important. The British were thin on the ground, and local talent had to be harnessed and trained to spread the burdens of responsibility, especially for dealing with problems that crossed state borders. Some sense of participation was gradually introduced and more was promised. In the Straits Settlements, more Eurasians, Chinese, Ceylonese and Indians were drawn in. In the Malay states under British control, educating the children of the Malay aristocracy and local elites was a small start. In the other Malay states, the British advisers helped the rulers to introduce regular training programmes for their younger officials.

MALAYA AS A STATE

The pace of change was slow and all plans came to naught when the tide of Japanese invasion swept across the region after

December 1941. British officials in London nursed the hurt of losing Singapore and began planning for a total restructuring of the Malaya to which they expected to return. Recognizing that the end of empire was nigh, the first step towards local self-government was to take "British" out of the name and simply use Malaya. The object was to create a Union comprised of the bitty parts and placed under a single system of government. When they returned, the British moved swiftly to use the renamed Malayan Union to replace the ungovernable cluster of polities that they had earlier created.

What kind of new political identity did the British have in mind for the future? For decades before the war, they had been resisting the anti-colonialism among Indians and Burmese, and also knew how their fellow imperialists were manipulating Indonesian and Vietnamese nationalist organizations. They were also aware that many of the nationalists received support from socialist and communist organizations in Europe and Soviet Russia. As for the large Chinese communities in Malaya, their hostile response to the Japanese invasion of China had drawn them deeply into China politics. British authorities had thousands of them under close surveillance and many were deported for activities contrary to British interests. But, by 1938, Europe was at war and Britain was threatened at home. There was little time to think about Malaya's future.

Historians agreed that the turning point for colonialism was when the Japanese seized all of the Malay Peninsula in 1941–42 from the world's largest empire. Japan had a different agenda and set out to reconstitute a different Malay world that would be pro-Japanese and anti-British. This required all those who identified with that Malay world to support the efforts to drive Western imperialists out. In addition, the Japanese suppressed all signs of nationalism among the local Chinese that were directed against them. In contrast, they engaged the Indians of the British army that had surrendered to them as well as local Indian youth to help them to rid Asia of imperialist domination. Consciously or not, they also demonstrated to the Malay elites whom they were wooing what could be done to Chinese nationalists and communists who opposed their ambitions.

The fall of Singapore thus marked the need for a new beginning. At the heart of the thinking was how to make Malaya a reality. The battle to redefine it became urgent. New parameters were spelt out in London, India, and among those awakened by the Japanese war. There was still the impulse to recover fresh credibility for the capitalist system. Against that were growing anti-colonial nationalisms and the arousal of primordial instincts that were ready to resort to violence.

First and foremost, Malaya needed a strong central bureaucratic state. Officials in London also came out with plans to develop an integrated Malayan economy. They were aware that this went against their earlier agreements with the Malay rulers but counted on the support of non-Malay communities who already accepted the idea of Malaya. They were also watchful of their former Malayan communist allies, some of whom they had armed and trained. In the end, they underestimated both the strength of the new Malay national consciousness and the pull of other nationalisms towards China, India and Indonesia. The result was that the hastily established Union had to be replaced by the Federation of Malaya. The new agreement made concessions to nationalists who wanted the constitutional rights of the Malay rulers guaranteed and strict limits set to citizenship rights for non-Malays.

The Federation of Malaya had from the start acute problems with all three themes that undergird that state: capital and labour; sound management; and political centralization. Capital was short after the war with the major developed economies struggling to revive. Labour unrest in the country was growing. The unrest was further dogged by communal tensions, especially between Chinese and Malays. This was in part a legacy of the discriminatory policies of the Japanese but aggravated by the fact that it was mainly the Chinese who led the Malayan Communist Party and the larger trade unions were in the hands of Chinese and Indians. By July 1948, a nationwide Emergency was declared and the country was in a state of war. As a result, investment capital became scarcer but labour troubles were brought under stricter control.[10] External conflicts in the region contributed to Malaya's economic difficulties but one of them, the Korean War in 1950, brought about a huge rise in demand for the country's rubber and enabled Malaya to prosper and recover from the very harsh years of the 1940s.

The country also lacked people with managerial skills. Initially, many people were recruited from abroad to run the new state. Investment in education was urgently needed and many training programmes were launched. In addition to commercial and industrial personnel, military and security manpower was also inadequate. The relative prosperity of the 1950s enabled developments to be nationwide and that hastened the desire for nationhood. With the Emergency war being won and administrative capacity improving in more areas, people were ready for the country's independence. It may be an exaggeration to say that a nation was being born but not wrong to declare that the task of nation building was in increasingly competent hands.

While the economy was picking up and the central administration gaining experience, the different communities were learning the art and tactics of national politics. With the security forces holding the ring during the worst years of the Emergency, new leaders emerged who thought and spoke in national terms. It is easy to forget how new this phenomenon was. Until then, most relationships were established within the boundaries of colony and state, with only a few British officials and some entrepreneurs acting beyond local borders. In the political arena, only the Malayan Communist Party leaders and a few anti-colonial teachers and journalists saw Malaya as the larger terrain and not merely a name. But the promise of nationhood was a spur to concerted action.

The British did their part to encourage elite participation to share responsibility and prepare for orderly succession when they left. At the heart of this was how to shape the contours of the Malayan nation. But the main action had to come from the national leaders themselves. How they could overcome the distance between communities and localities quickly and effectively so that more people could believe in their shared destiny. In short, beyond the centralization of the state machinery, there was the challenging task to make Malaya something real to everyone.

In 1962, I published an essay that defined *Malayan* nationalism as having two component parts: a nucleus of Malay nationalism enclosed by the idea of Malay-Chinese-Indian partnership. The Malaya Federation had been around since 1948 and I found it possible to identify its meaning. When I wrote that, the Prime Minister had launched the new Malaysia project. I was confident that the definition would survive the name-change. I saw that the Malay determination to rule over Tanah Melayu would not change.[11] The entry of Singapore, Sarawak and Sabah into the equation would give more time for Malaya to shade into Tanah Melayu, but the Malay core would remain in the new Malaysia.

MALAYA AS PLATFORM

As explained in the previous chapter, Malaysia and Singapore each went its own way after 1965. The two large northern Borneo states remained in Malaysia but without the help of the politically more experienced leaders of Singapore. During the negotiations, Sarawak and Sabah obtained favourable terms to take account of the fact that the majority of their indigenous peoples were not Muslim, and they were given the rights of *pribumi* similar to those of the Malays. Thus they shared some of the characteristics of the plural society that guided the politics on the peninsula, and their representation in the parliament was strong and reassuring.

On the surface, the larger new federation appeared to proceed as if the Federation of Malaya had expanded across the South China Sea, and Malaya served as a platform for the new state. The ruling party, reconstituted as a National Front (Barisan National, BN), was fully in charge and set out to socialize the young parties in Sarawak and Sabah to embrace the methods that they had adopted. The BN was also successful in structuring the bureaucratic system to support the constitutional rights of the Malay sultanate, measures that had moved the country closer to the ideal of Tanah Melayu. In that context, the name-change enabled the Malay community to take the new name of Malaysia as an English rendering of Tanah Melayu. That way, it could notionally move away from the Malaya idea that the British imagined and the non-Malays preferred.

There were matters that are differently understood between West and East Malaysia. For example, Malaya consisted of eleven states whose positions were more or less equal. If Malaysia were an extension of Malaya, adding two states makes it a country of thirteen comparable states. By agreement, however, Sarawak and Sabah have rights that the other states do not have and can, in practice, act as if they were in a federation of three states, West Malaysia, Sarawak and Sabah. For the central government, the concessions made at the time Malaysia was established in 1963 were part of a transitional arrangement, whereas many in the Borneo states insist that these terms should remain in place. In practice, what was agreed has enabled the two states to protect their labour force and their investment interests, train a local bureaucracy in managerial skills, and thus strengthen state administration at all levels. And insofar as the East Malaysians have control of the local political arena, their exceptional position has given them advantages that they are unlikely to give up.

Therefore, Malaysia has not necessarily been a simple extension of Malaya and could be seen to be sufficiently different to be a fresh start in nation building. It is still too early to say if a new kind of nation will materialize that is neither Malaya nor Tanah Melayu. But, for the past fifty years, the processes of development in the new federation are remarkably similar to those that were evolved in the eleven states of Malaya between 1948 and 1963. Taking the three themes the British and the Malayan federal government paid close attention to when designing the Malaya they wanted — capital and labour, sound management, and centralization — it can be said that Malaysia has used Malaya as a platform and its development has followed the same trajectory. During a half century of major shifts in global trade and unexpected changes to security structures, to pursue those three objectives with relative success is no mean feat. It reflects the mastery of the modern technologies imparted via the colonial state and further developed in Malaya by adaptive skills and local innovation during the formative years before Malaysia was born. Despite the differences in demography, cultures and protective zones when the Borneo states joined the federation, the peninsular experiences of the first two-thirds of the twentieth century provided great assists to the larger federation during the last third. By the twenty-first century, the population as a whole shared so much together that it would be true to say that the key strengths that Malaya had started with have now grown to fill the Malaysia spaces.

The Malay leadership put new flesh on a British-proposed skeleton that suited their agenda. They may be said not to have lost sight of their goal of reshaping Malaya into a form of Tanah Melayu. The genius was in the constitutional framework agreed on that put in place a stable four-legged structure of monarchy, *bangsa*-centred bureaucracy, primacy of Islam and acceptance of a plural society. As long as the four legs were equal, stability could be assured.[12] And it would be fair to say that the efforts to maintain that equality were widely appreciated.

In that context, the four years of disputation between 1961 and 1965 about the nature of the new federation were unsettling. There was serious questioning of the structure, in part by Singapore, supported by new leaders in northern Borneo, and in part by those Malay leaders who had not been satisfied with the Malaya formula. After Singapore's separation, the Malaya idea had lost its momentum. The Barisan government's attempts to redefine Malaysia satisfied neither those who wanted to affirm the Malaya structure nor those who dreamt of Tanah Melayu. The results of the 1969 elections brought this to a head, followed by riots and, for many, what seemed like the end of an era.[13]

Developments since then under a much stronger UMNO leadership have included striking innovations and modifications to earlier practices, notably a deliberate moving away from British ways to "Look East", that were seen as departures from the Malaya ideal. Other creative changes were also significant. They were largely in response to the new Islamic awakening, to dissatisfaction with the privileges of the constitutional monarchy, and to greater divisiveness among the non-Malay communities. Taken together, this weakened the quadrilateral balance that seemed secure before 1963. By the turn of the century, the two legs of central bureaucracy and Islam were clearly more equal than the other two, and growing instability has dogged all political activity ever since.

The reasons for the recent turn of events are complex. At its heart would seem to have been the changeover after 1969 from the Malaya model to that of Tanah Melayu–Malaysia. That was further challenged when resurgent Islam took successfully to politics. The failure to deal with the financial crisis of the late 1990s accompanied by bloated corruption contributed to the loss of political credibility of the major parties.[14]

In the midst of the new uncertainties, many of the ideas and institutions rooted in the Federation of Malaya of 1948–61 have endured. The desire for good governance is strong and the language demanding it is still there. The calls for integrity, responsibility and transparency continue to be made. Democratic rhetoric and processes remain little changed. At least, faith in their relevance seems to be strong. Sometimes, I hear notes of despair but the aspirations of those who believe that reform is possible are widespread and positive. Despite the tensions in the air, efforts at maintaining communal harmony are sincere, plans for economic growth are expertly drawn and, on the whole, civil control at the centre remains confident and relatively impartial. In short, the structure laid down in Malaya is more or less intact even though the character of some of the leading figures in government looks badly flawed. This suggests that it was never intended for the Malaya model to be replaced when Malaysia came into being. The failures stem from problems of political ambition, of policy implementation, of new wealth and greed, all aggravated by the country's openness to external security and ideological pressures. However, if the quadrilateral structure is only temporarily unbalanced, and regaining the necessary balance is possible, the transition from Malaya to Malaysia as Tanah Melayu could be said to be still in progress.

This perspective of what happened in Malaysia may be compared with the road taken by Singapore after independence. In some ways, separation marked a sharp break with the Malaya that it had waited to join since at least when the Malayan Union left it out in 1946, if not since the Japanese separated Syonan from Ma-rai-ee in February 1942. Although separately governed, it had been closely connected with the destiny of Malaya. Its people were aware of the Tanah Melayu agenda implicit in the Federation when that Malaya became independent in 1957. But its open questioning of that agenda made it impossible for it to remain in Malaysia. Thus it is not surprising that, after 1965, Singapore would have less in common with Malaysia than before. The small city-state not only had to survive but also had to make its neighbours treat it with respect as an equal. It had to learn to deal with an unstable region by reaching out further to find security and generate economic growth. Under the circumstances, republican Singapore seemed to have moved out of the Malaya orbit altogether.

But, significantly, where the plural society was concerned, the Singapore leaders reaffirmed that port-city heritage, probably one of its most important, from the colonial state. This was a vital link with one of the assumptions underlying British Malaya and the Malayan Union. That tied it closely to the key themes of development that the British had pursued during the first half of the twentieth century. I return to the issues of capital and labour, sound management and centralization. Clearly, the first two were essential if the city-state was to endure.

The first called for openness to global markets and access to talent, to providing education and training based on principles of meritocracy and to ensuring that the investors and their workers worked in an atmosphere of trust. The second required competent and dedicated civil servants equipped to manage a city-state that could navigate in a competitive world of entrepreneurship, one dependent on rapidly changing technologies. For that, a credible legal system served as the foundation. As for the third, spatial and administrative centralization was not the issue. What was crucial was the defence of the state's physical security and the maintenance of social harmony among its multicultural population. For that, legitimacy and power were central.

Singapore's success the past five decades has largely been attributed to the presence of all three themes in its development. What has not been stressed is that all three originated from the Malaya model. The country has, of course, made innovative changes in governance and has advanced its goals more systematically than ever before and prospered as a result. In other words, it is not only the plural society that ties it to the Malaya heritage. It is also the larger global frame that Singapore as the great port of Malaya was designed to serve. What had made the difference was the sense of danger, the creativity prodded by paranoia, with which the city-state approached the perilous conditions that awaited it in 1965.

CONCLUSION

The British did not set out to create an independent Malaya. Singapore was a product in part of the India–China trade and in part of the Napoleonic wars in Europe. British officials and businesses in the Straits Settlements later intervened in the Malay States in the 1870s, and the additional states led to the name of

Malaya. About the turn of the century, it became convenient to include the three settlements in that name. For the next decades to 1941, this Malaya was centred in Singapore, with a few more states awkwardly placed in a semi-formal relationship with that centre. By 1946, one Malaya officially excluded Singapore and acquired its association with Tanah Melayu while another popularly included Singapore in a future Malaya that would be free of colonialism. But when independence finally came in 1957, Singapore was left out. Malaya then became the platform for building the Malayan nation. Singapore waited its turn. It was brought into Malaysia but was soon asked to leave.

I have suggested above that the Malaysia with the Borneo states was torn between being different and becoming a more Malay Malaya, one now enlarged. This is still contentious and the nature of the future Malaysian nation is yet to be agreed on. But what has kept this federation together is the way its elites have used Malaya as a platform for nation building. Despite the national emergency after the riots of 1969, there seem not to have been an alternative to that platform. New policies were introduced, some constitutional amendments were made and real political power was redistributed. But the basis for national development followed the Malaya trajectory more or less successfully. That can be identified as Malaya platform A, one that serves to mark out the nation-state path.

Singapore chose to base its city-state on a plural society built on principles of meritocracy and secularism and did not expect its peoples to conform to a Chinese identity. This meant that it turned away from the nationalism founded on ethnic majority power. It thus distanced itself from the Tanah Melayu element in the Malaya model. On the other hand, making that choice brought it closer to the Malaya imaginary that the British started out with and pursued until they agreed to accept the modified terms of nationhood that the Federation of Malaya leaders wanted. Although Singapore's leaders are committed to build a nation, they understand that that has to be for the long haul. More urgently, the city-state needed employment and a sense of security and they stayed with the themes of growth, management and central power that Malaya had stood for. The challenges they faced made them seek a larger role in the international order. The ambition to become a global city has taken Singapore well beyond what Malaya sought to be. That has led it to use Malaya creatively as another kind of platform, one that can be called Malaya platform B, one that helped the Singapore leaders secure the city-state path.

I do not know how long the two Malaya platforms A and B will serve Malaysia and Singapore each in their different ways. When the founding leaders chose their separate paths, they acted on political differences that they thought were unbridgeable. But they had lived through a shared Malayan set of ideas and institutions that had, by 1965, been around for decades. They could not in the end shed that heritage, nor did they particularly want to. Two generations later, it is still possible to recognize the roles that the Malaya platforms have played. It leads us to consider, even when nation and city ambitions draw the peoples apart, why their pursuit of success has features that are traceable to the Malaya ideal that the two countries had once consciously shared.

Notes

1. A few Malays did use Malaya, for example, in the Parti Kebangsaan Melayu Malaya (PKMM, Malay Nationalist Party of Malaya), as a step towards a future Melayu Raya (Malaya with Indonesia), but that was a transitional political term and was temporary. Ariffin Omar, *Bangsa Melayu: Malay concepts of democracy and community, 1945–1950* (Kuala Lumpur: Oxford University Press, 1993); Syed

Muhd Khairuddin Aljunied, *Radicals: Resistance and protest in colonial Malaya* (DeKalb: Northern Illinois Press, 2015).

2. The name Syonan was used in Singapore in 2017 for a gallery to remind people of the atrocities of war. This evoked painful memories among older Singaporeans and led to the dramatic name-change announced on 17 February to revert to its old name of "Former Ford Factory". But, apart from the bitter memories, there was particular significance in the name-change from Singapore to Syonan because the Japanese did not change any other city-name to a Japanese name in all the territories they occupied in 1942–45. That meant that, while supporting anti-colonial movements elsewhere in the Malay world, they had hoped to keep Singapore-Syonan as headquarters of their virtual empire in the South. <http://www.straitstimes.com/singapore/war-gallery-name-change-a-timeline>.

3. I was born in Surabaya and therefore had to apply to be naturalized as a Federal citizen; I qualified because I had lived in Malaya for at least 15 of 20 years before my application.

4. Malayan had come to be popularly used only after the end of World War II. It became official and was used mostly by non-Malays during the Malayan Union in 1946, James de V. Allen, *The Malayan Union* (New Haven: Yale University Southeast Asian Studies, 1967); Albert Lau, *The Malayan Union controversy 1942–1948* (Singapore: Oxford University Press South-East Asian historical monographs series, 1990). As far as I can remember, only the very few English-educated Malays might use Malayan in certain contexts but most Malays always used Melayu.

5. Loh Kah Seng, Edgar Liao, Cheng Tju Lim and Seng Guo Quan, *The University Socialist Club and the contest for Malaya: Tangled strands of modernity*, IIAS Publications Series, Monograph no. 7 (Amsterdam: Amsterdam University Press, 2012); Poh Soo Kai, Tan Jing Quee and Koh Kay Yew, eds, *The Fajar Generation: The University Socialist Club and the politics of Postwar Malaya and Singapore* (Petaling Jaya: Strategic Information and Research Development Centre, 2010).

6. Mahathir bin Mohamad, *The Malay dilemma* (Singapore: Times Books

International, 1970); Lee Ting Hui, *Chinese schools in British Malaya: Policies and politics* (Singapore: South Seas Society, 2006); Tan Jing Quee, Tan Kok Chiang and Lysa Hong, eds, *The May 13 Generation: The Chinese Middle Schools Student Movement and Singapore politics in the 1950s* (Petaling Jaya: Strategic Information and Research Development Centre, 2011). My Anderson School classmate, Aminuddin Baki, also fellow student at University of Malaya, and another fellow student at university, Mahathir Mohamad, both told me that one would have to be active outside the campus to have any impact on national consciousness. Others pointed to the Chinese high school students in Singapore to underline the point.

7. Hugh Clifford was freely using Malaya and Malayan by 1900, while Frank Swettenham, *British Malaya: An account of the origins and progress of British influence in Malaya* (London: J. Lane, Bodley Head, 1907), was authoritative. Widely distributed at the Malaya Pavilion at the British Empire exhibition was *Illustrated Guide to British Malaya*, published in Kuala Lumpur, 1924. Richard Winstedt's edited book was published in London by Constable in 1923.

8. Cheah Boon Kheng, ed., *From PKI to the Comintern, 1924–1941: The apprenticeship of the Malayan Communist Party — Selected documents and discussion* (Ithaca: Cornell University Southeast Asia Program, 1992); Volume 1 of the two-volume collection of Chinese papers pertaining to the Malayan Communist Party, edited by the 21st Century Publishers in Kuala Lumpur, 《战前地下斗争时期》. 吉隆坡: 21世纪出版社, 2010, vol. 1, 建党初期阶段; and the published interviews with Eu Chooi Yip from the Singapore Oral History Archives, edited by Chen Jian 陈剑:《浪尖逐梦――余柱业口述历史档案》 [Oral History Memoirs] (Petaling Jaya: Strategic Information and Research Development Centre, 2006).

9. Yeo Kim Wah, *Politics of decentralization: Colonial controversy in Malaya 1920–1929* (Kuala Lumpur: Oxford University Press, 1982).

10. Charles Gamba, *The origins of trade unionism in Malaya: A study in colonial labour unrest* (Singapore: Donald Moore for Eastern Universitites Press, 1962); Michael Stenson, *Industrial conflict in*

Malaya: Prelude to the Communist revolt of 1948 (London: Oxford University Press, 1970). Also, Chin Peng, *My side of history*, as told to Ian Ward and Norma Miraflor (Singapore: Media Masters, 2003).

11. "Malayan Nationalism", *Royal Central Asian Journal*, vol. 49, pts. iii and iv (London, 1962), later reprinted in *Community and Nation: Essays on Southeast Asia and China,* selected and edited by Anthony Reid (Kuala Lumpur and Sydney: Heinemann Asia and Allen & Unwin, 1981).

12. Wang Gungwu, "Reflections on Malaysian Elites", *Review of Indonesian and Malay Studies* 20, no. 1 (1986), Sydney, reprinted in 2nd edition of *Community and Nation: China, Southeast Asia and Australia,* 1992.

13. Goh Cheng Teik, *The May thirteenth incident and democracy in Malaysia* (Kuala Lumpur: Oxford University Press, 1971); Leon Comber, *13 May 1969: The darkest day in Malaysian history* (Singapore: Marshall Cavendish Editions, 2009).

14. Cheah Boon Kheng, *Malaysia: The making of a nation* (Singapore: Institute of Southeast Asian Studies, 2002).

PART TWO

Locality in Flux

Chapter 4

REMEMBERING GOH KENG SWEE

I first met Goh Keng Swee in London in the mid-1950s at meetings in Malaya Hall and remember the occasions when he talked about the future of an independent Malaya. We met again after I returned in 1957 to teach at the University of Malaya in Singapore and he invited me occasionally to lunch to talk about the Malaya that had just become independent. We agreed that it was only a matter of time when Singapore will also be independent. We talked about the factors that kept Singapore and the Federation apart and saw that the British wanted their colony to serve their trading and strategic purposes for as long as possible. We met informally a few more times and even talked about what a Malayan identity might be like. I also recall moments when we touched on the question of being overseas Chinese in Malaya and Singapore and what the rise of China could mean to their lives.[1]

When the University of Malaya established its Kuala Lumpur campus in 1959, I volunteered to teach there. Dr Goh understood that as my way of continuing to prepare for the day when the two territories became one country. The efforts to establish a new federation called Malaysia began soon afterwards. From 1959 till the separation in 1965, I visited Singapore several times. Some of my trips had to do with preparing the volume of essays, *Malaysia:*

A Survey (1964) that I was editing.[2] Others were made after I was appointed in 1964 by Singapore's Minister for Education, Ong Pang Boon, to chair the Nanyang University Curriculum Review Committee. This was to make recommendations concerning the university's future in the new Malaysian Federation.[3] Yet others were for me to give lectures in the old campus, now renamed the University of Singapore while the division in Kuala Lumpur retained the Malaya name. During some of these visits, I saw Dr Goh and he was interested to hear my views of the new country from a KL perspective.

After separation and the republic's independence, he asked to see me in 1967 about the establishment of the Institute of Southeast Asian Studies and outlined his plans to build a centre that would help Singapore understand the region and be at the same time a research institution of international repute. What struck me most about that meeting was his insistence that the institute not be a part of government. Although he was Minister for Defence, he was particularly concerned that the institute's staff should not think like department officials trying to solve the kinds of problems that each department believed would need urgent attention. What he wanted, he told me, were well-trained and proven scholars who could analyse problems in depth and take a longer view. They must be able to identify current issues and trends but would study how these had arisen and examine the kinds of consequences that could follow. Dr Goh also believed that the best way for the institute to contribute to Singapore's relations with its neighbours was to attract top researchers in the field whether from the region or from the best centres anywhere in the world. He underlined the importance of not having the institute being seen as merely servicing the government or any of its agencies but as a body of learned scholars alert to current changes that could look ahead at future developments.

What he had in mind was brilliantly thought through. I was excited by his plans and strongly supported his visionary enterprise but, having accepted appointment to the Chair of Far Eastern History at the Australian National University, I was not able to join it. Nevertheless, I kept in close touch for the next thirty years with successive directors, Harry Benda, John Legge, Josef Silverstein and Kernial Singh Sandhu, and was delighted when, in 1995, Director Chan Heng Chee invited me to join ISEAS in a research capacity.

After I moved to Canberra in 1968, I had no direct contact with Dr Goh for many years until 1982. That year, I spent several months as Visiting Professor in the History Department of the National University of Singapore. He was then Minister for Education and Deputy Prime Minister. He was interested in two issues in the schools, the teaching of ethics and a new history curriculum. He asked to see me about them both. When we discussed the question of the teaching of Confucian ethics, I offered my views about doing that in public schools. He noted my doubts but was determined to proceed.

When we talked about the teaching of history, he invited me to advise the Ministry on a new curriculum for secondary schools. I recommended a Singapore perspective on a wide range of regional and global events that had affected Singapore's development. I advised that innovative teaching methods would have to be found to encourage pupils to be curious about how the many pasts of a plural society could influence their lives as Singapore citizens.

TWO INSTITUTES

It was not until 1993 that I had the chance to see Dr Goh again. As Vice-Chancellor of the University of Hong Kong, I had the privilege of hosting him when he came to HKU to receive his Honorary Doctorate of Letters. By that time, the Cold War had ended and China was changing fast. We talked about developments in China and the advice he was giving to the Chinese government on their new Special Economic Zones. He updated me about the work of the Institute of East Asian Political Economy (IEAPE) that he established in 1992 and explained what he hoped it could do to help Singapore play a role in China's future.[4] Little did I know that I would one day have a close relationship with that institute.

After I announced that I planned to retire from HKU in 1995, Director Chan Heng Chee of the Institute of Southeast Asian Studies (now ISEAS – Yusof Ishak Institute) asked me not to return to the Australian National University (ANU) immediately but to do some research and writing in Singapore. My wife Margaret, who grew up in Singapore, was also very keen that we spend some time there. But before I could take up that position, I received a letter from Dr Goh inviting me to succeed him as executive chairman of the IEAPE. The move to Singapore now became quite irresistible. I had no idea that it would be the beginning of a relationship with the two institutes that was to continue for over twenty years.

We arrived in Singapore early in January 1996. Although I reported for duty in both institutes, it was understood that taking over the IEAPE had priority because Dr Goh had expressed his wish to retire. My ISEAS project on nation building was temporarily set aside while I concentrated on attracting more academically trained scholars to IEAPE. The institute was in an advantageous position. Although it did not have a formal link with the National University of Singapore (NUS), it had a set of rooms in the Faculty of Arts and Social Sciences building. The Director John Wong who had joined the original Institute of East Asian Philosophies from the Department of Economics was helping to change the institute's research direction. As founder and former Chairman, Dr Goh stayed on to help me steer the Institute while I settled in.

I discovered that, unlike ISEAS, IEAPE was registered as a limited company. Dr Goh established it to concentrate on China's domestic developments and not do what most other China institutes wrote about, which was to focus on China's relations with other powers. He also did not want the institute to be the kind of think-tank that advocated, or commented on, policies and was designed to help government and other interest groups draw up policies. He believed that the institute would best serve the public and private sectors in Singapore if it could provide accurate and up-to-date facts about the developments within China. To do this at a credible level, it had to attract research scholars who could collect and analyse reliable data and produce materials that were policy relevant.

The team that he had put together included scholars of contemporary China developments as well as people with direct experience of governance and policymaking in China. Dr Goh and John Wong had shown them how to write the kind of papers that could help Singapore institutions understand what was rapidly changing in China. We spoke about how to recruit scholars who not only have an intimate understanding of contemporary China but have also mastered the kinds of methodologies needed to determine what is actually happening and explain the significance of those developments. We found that recruiting people with such skills was more difficult than expected. We explored the reasons why the institute was not attracting people with the necessary background and why we were not getting more applications from the kinds of scholars we needed.

Vice-Chancellor Professor Lim Pin was very keen to have the institute as part of NUS. This encouraged Dr Goh to explore that prospect with other key stakeholders. It was decided that I take over as Director and I was delighted when John Wong agreed to stay on and be the institute's research director. The institute was also fortunate to retain the services of scholars like Zheng Yongnian who had joined us. Dr Goh then took formal steps, with government backing, to enable the endowment funds of the company to be transferred to the NUS exclusively for the use of the autonomous institute. The Deputy Prime Minister Tony Tan Keng Yam (later President of the Republic) and Professor Lim Pin had a meeting with me and John Wong to be assured that the transfer would be satisfactory to all concerned. The transfer formalities then began.

I proposed that the institute be renamed the East Asian Institute (EAI) to broaden its coverage although we still intended that the main focus of its research should remain that of the political economy of China and the impact of China's development on its neighbours. Professor Lim was happy to have this first social science institute to become part of the NUS and was very helpful with all the logistics issues involved in the transfer. The NUS established a Management Board consisting of three Deans (of the Faculties of Arts and Social Sciences, Law, and the Business School) and three Permanent Secretaries (of Foreign Affairs, Trade and Industry, and Defence) with Hsuan Owyang, a former banker who had led the growth of Singapore's renowned Housing Development Board, as its Chairman. The Deans were asked to help the institute recruit research staff and monitor the institute's academic performance. The Permanent Secretaries would ensure that the institute's work could deal with their concerns as well as become useful and relevant to the community. I was particularly grateful for the arrangement whereby the institute's library became a discrete part of the NUS Library system but remained with us for the use of the institute's research staff.

When all that was done, NUS invited Minister for Information and the Arts George Yeo to relaunch the institute in its new academic home. With the university's support, the institute was able to attract the specialist researchers we needed. By being in academia, the scholars worked hard to bridge the gap between research and public education that Dr Goh wanted us to do. His injunction to be up-to-date and accurate has guided the institute's work ever since.

The two institutions through which Dr Goh and I reconnected after working in cities far apart, ISEAS since 1967 and EAI since 1996, paralleled the way Singapore was responding to rapidly changing times. ISEAS was born when the former colony and a key part of Malaysia had unexpectedly become an independent state. And this happened in a Southeast Asia in the grips of the fiercest anti-colonial war the region has ever seen, in the struggle for the reunification of Vietnam. It was also after a failed coup that led to the fall of Sukarno and rise of Suharto in Indonesia. Clearly, it was urgent that the Singapore government and its people should have an accurate understanding of the neighbouring new nations. By the time I arrived in 1996, enough time had passed for us to think about an historical accounting of the various early experiences in nation building. Successive directors of ISEAS, Chan Heng Chee, Chia Siow Yue and K. Kesavapany, all supported the project, and the ISEAS project eventually published four volumes in the History of Nation-Building Series.[5]

The creation of IEAPE (later renamed the EAI) was no less urgent. Singapore had finally established formal relations with China after decades of keeping a safe distance from its several revolutions. This China was clearly committed to turn around and engage with the global market economy. In its eyes, Singapore's system of government and maritime networks were clearly of growing importance. Dr Goh quickly realized that there were serious gaps in Singapore's so far indirect knowledge of this China and that the government and public had depended too much on the Western media and other agencies of the Cold War era for much of their information and analysis. He identified China's transformation under Deng Xiaoping as a historical turning point not only for China but also for the region to its south. It was therefore essential for Singapore to have its own direct and independent capacity to understand what is happening, especially within that huge and complex country. The IEAPE/EAI was the first of many centres to keep things up-to-date in order to prepare Singapore to be more deeply engaged with China's future developments.

THE MAN I KNEW

Dr Goh's life took him from the travails of the British and Japanese empires to the uncertain paths of Singapore's independence. There then arose an unfamiliar Southeast Asian regional consciousness and the surprising speed of China's re-emergence of as a global economic power. He responded quickly and acted decisively to remedy whatever was lacking in the newborn city-state. In the course of doing that, he reminded us of the deep ties between China and the region and the rich possibilities for all if the two worked out the right relationship for the future. His agility of mind was legend.

I have followed Dr Goh's public life mostly from afar and read reports of how he built a robust economy, a defence-alert community and a knowledge-centred nation. Remarkably, he was widely admired for his innovative methods. For myself, I respected him most for his immense intellectual curiosity. He had a scholarly approach to every problem, seeking to be objective and thorough so that policy decisions were always based on reliable information.

When Dr Goh joined the People's Action Party's first cabinet as Minister for Finance, no one was surprised. He was well known as a brilliant economics scholar and no one doubted that he would give Singapore a carefully thought-through plan to overcome the many disadvantages it faced as a small state that had never prepared to go it alone. In the context of Malaysia, those of us who were in Kuala Lumpur were interested in the fact that he had to negotiate with his cousin Tan Siew Sin, his counterpart in the Federation government. It was well known that he defended Singapore's special concerns with utmost vigour.

After Singapore separated from Malaysia, and Dr Goh became Defence Minister, I was surprised how much he was able to achieve in this realm. It was truly impressive what the new armed forces of this young country had become in only a few years. Much later, when his daughter-in-law, Tan Siok San, invited me to write a foreword for her biography of him, I was struck by something he wrote when he was only 13 years old. It so astonished me that I quoted it in my foreword,

> ... China needs engineers, scientists, inventors and sailors badly. She has not a respectable navy and air force.... China needs soldiers, sailors and airmen to help her become one of the best nations in the world..."[6]

What he wished China to become seems almost prescient not only of what he helped Singapore to become but also of his role as adviser to China at a historic turn of its modern history. It can also be seen as the backdrop to why he was keen to build a research institute that would monitor how China could one day become "one of the best nations".

At Dr Goh's funeral in 2010, I was reminded of one of our conversations when we talked about the region's history. He talked about how the various Chinese communities were formed in the region, especially in Malaya, and what needed to be done to get them to share a common understanding of their future in Southeast Asia. This was also the occasion when we talked about our very different family backgrounds. He came from a Malacca Baba family and was conscious of how Chinese lived with Malays for centuries. He had grown up being sensitive about the concerns of the Malay world. He had read carefully about their maritime empires and their rise and fall, how they were doing quite well until the eighteenth century when, following the industrial revolution in Europe, that world was transformed. We talked about how, when Singapore was founded, Malay power was at its weakest. He was interested to know what it would be like when Malay-ness returned as a force.

In that context, he was curious about the underlying nature of Chinese history. We began talking about this when he discussed my background. My parents had come from China, both descended from literati families that had undergone traumatic experiences after the fall of the Qing dynasty and the end of the Confucian state. My father was steeped in classical learning but later studied in a modern university. At the university, he grew to love English literature and mastered the language so that he could better appreciate it in the language in which it was written.

My father then joined hundreds of others who went to the Nanyang to teach young Chinese in the island world of Southeast Asia. Because he was a university graduate, he was eventually recruited to work in the British-administered Malay state of Perak as an inspector of Chinese schools. I explained how he had prepared me to study in his alma mater in Nanjing, but after the China he knew and loved came under Mao Zedong's Communist Party, he sent me to study in the University of Malaya. He advised me that I should now prepare to live in the maritime world in which I was born.

On one occasion, I told Dr Goh that my father knew his uncle, Tan Cheng Lock, and was together in the same meeting hall in Ipoh when the Communists tried to assassinate Tan Cheng Lock, then the leader of the Malayan Chinese Association. This led him to ask whether my father really accepted the idea that a Baba like Tan Cheng Lock could lead the Chinese community, especially one that was largely China-born. Actually, my father admired some of the outstanding Baba of the time. He had earlier met Dr Lim Boon Keng and thought very highly of his scholarship and many achievements. He was particularly impressed by the way the Baba community remained Chinese for centuries despite living in alien environments.

I first met people of Baba background as a schoolboy in Ipoh, and saw how they were torn between their local cultural links and their desire to be seen as Chinese. I felt keen sympathy for the predicament of my school friends when Chinese nationalism was at its strongest during the Sino-Japanese War. It made me more sensitive to what lay behind the idea of Chinese identity. Learning about their lives also enriched my reading of Chinese history and helped me to understand the role of the strong cultures that shaped China through the ages. Meeting and getting to know Dr Goh provided me with new dimensions of appreciation of their role in history for which I am most grateful.

Notes

1. I have benefitted greatly from reading Tan Siok Sun, *Goh Keng Swee: A Portrait* (Singapore: Editions Didier Millet, 2007), and Ooi Kee Beng, *In lieu of ideology: The intellectual biography of Goh Keng Swee* (Singapore: Institute of Southeast Asian Studies, 2010).

    Some of my earlier views on Dr Goh may be found in the foreword to a new edition of his *Wealth of East Asian Nations*, edited by Linda Low (Singapore: Marshall Cavendish Academic, 2004), pp. vii–viii;

also in the foreword to Tan Siok Sun's biography, pp. 6–9. When Barry Desker and Kwa Chong Guan edited a memorial volume dedicated to him, I gave an interview about the years I have known him, from the 1950s to my joining the Institute of East Asian Political Economy (IEAPE). A part of that was included in *Goh Keng Swee: A Public Career Remembered* (Singapore: World Scientific and S. Rajaratnam School of International Studies, NTU, and National Archives, 2012), pp. 156–59.

2. *Malaysia: A Survey* (New York and London: Praeger and Pall Mall Press, 1964), 466 pp.

3. As Chairman of the Nanyang University Review Committee that prepared *Report of the Nanyang University Review Committee* (Singapore Nanyang University, 42 pp., 1965). (南洋大学课程审查委员会报告书, collected in 王如明主编《南洋大学文献: 南洋大学创办六十周年纪念: 一九五五年至二〇一五年》新加坡: 新加坡南洋大学毕业生协会, 2015.)

4. For a fuller story of his role in the early history of the EAI, see *The East Asian Institute: A Goh Keng Swee Legacy* (Singapore: World Scientific, 2016).

5. Cheah Boon Kheng, *Malaysia: The Making of a Nation* (2002); Wang Gungwu, ed., *Nation-building: Five Southeast Asian Histories* (2005); Edwin Lee, *Singapore: The Unexpected Nation* (2008) and Taufik Abdullah, *Indonesia: Towards Democracy* (2009). All were published by ISEAS, the Institute's great asset for all those who study Southeast Asia's rich history and culture, and its unceasing efforts to build a regional presence in world affairs.

6. Tan Siok Sun, *Goh Keng Swee: A Portrait*, pp. 7–11.

Chapter 5

BEFORE NATION
Chinese Peranakan

The many studies of the Baba or Chinese Peranakan of the three cities of the former Straits Settlements have provided us with an intriguing picture of a wonderfully distinct community. At the first international conference on Chinese Peranakan, I congratulated the organizers for taking the initiative to broaden the subject beyond the Malay peninsula. I also thought that what made the conference special was the way it honoured Tun Tan Cheng Lock who was one of the most important Peranakan Chinese of the twentieth century.[1] He is remembered for his many contributions

This chapter is a slightly revised version of the keynote lecture given at the conference on "Peranakan Chinese in a Globalizing Southeast Asia: The Case of Singapore, Malaysia and Indonesia", held in Singapore on 22 May 2009. It was published as "The Peranakan Phenomenon: Pre-national, Marginal, and Transnational", in *Peranakan Chinese in a Globalizing Southeast Asia*, edited by Leo Suryadinata (Singapore: Chinese Heritage Centre and National University of Singapore Museum Baba House, 2010), pp. 14–26.

The French translation was published as "Le phenomene peranakan", in *La Culture Peranakan: Guide A-Z* (Singapore: Asian Civilisations Museum, 2010), pp. 17–29.

to the history of Malaya. His story, not only his leadership of Peranakan but also his success in providing a bridge between Peranakan and other Chinese, as well as between Chinese and Malays and other communities of Malaysia, was a remarkable achievement. When fully told, the story would provide us with a better sense of what the Peranakan phenomenon means for those who inherited that heritage.

I had from young seen the community largely from afar, but in the last decade, I have read some remarkable studies and become more familiar with the Singapore community as it is. This has helped me understand how the community has been developing. For example, the TV shows, the revival of certain parts of the culture and, most of all, the historic establishment of the Peranakan Museum.[2] Some years ago, before the opening of the museum, I had the privilege to be invited by the Peranakan Association to talk about "the Peranakan in a global setting", a topic close to the theme of this conference. At that talk, I concentrated on some features of the community that had attracted my attention. I spoke about the strength of the Peranakan family and the role of the women, especially their roles as mothers, and the effect of time and place on those who grew up in Peranakan families. I looked at the life choices made by individual Peranakan, the consequences of those choices on their later lives, and also about how they kept their identity differently from most other Chinese spread around the world.

Since that talk, there have been many changes in things Peranakan. I went back recently to have another look at the Peranakan Museum, to admire the artefacts and the display of historical sensibilities that raised new questions about the community's extraordinary story. Museums do not only tell us about what happened in the past, or help us study about the past. Good curators of museums can also inspire new ideas and values, fresh ways of looking at people of the past, but also new ways of looking at people today. Returning to this topic after several years, other perspectives have come to mind, and I want to share them with you. These include ideas that have led me to the broader issue of what I call the Peranakan phenomenon.

THE PERANAKAN PHENOMENON

The Peranakan could be described as a proto-national community that was to have an influence on Chinese notions of state and nation. I refer to the fact that they were the first Chinese community to be given a distinct identity in jurisdictions administered in the name of two of the world's earliest nation-states, the Dutch and the English. Thus the Peranakan felt the impact of those national interests before the Chinese in China became aware of the idea of nationhood. Their status as Chinese in the colonial context provided them with something akin to a "national" identity in the eyes of the Dutch and British who knew what that meant.[3] It defined for them a space that was proto-national.

At the beginning of the twentieth century, the Peranakan experienced marginalization during an era of nation building by both Chinese and indigenous nationalist leaders, some of whom could not decide whether or not they should be included in that process. For most of them, China was divided, and its weak condition also impacted on the community's self-image and inflicted among them degrees of doubt about whom they were. Today, many members of the community have chosen new identities but it is still pertinent to ask what trajectories are possible for them as Chinese power grows markedly in an increasingly transnational environment. As a student of Chinese history, I am interested in this phenomenon because it helps us understand how people consider themselves Chinese and why, when and where they do not. Such changes obviously depend on a range of different circumstances, and charting the changes could help us look at the future of existing Peranakan communities, consider whether there can be new kinds of Peranakan, and also ask what other Peranakan-like phenomenon might emerge in the future.

The point is that the phenomenon is more than of mere historical interest. It is singularly significant in at least one major way. Since the eighteenth century, the community as a proto-national entity has grown and adapted to changes for over 200 years. We can see six stages in their efforts to survive and reinvent themselves as such a proto-national community. Let me outline the six stages here.

PRE-NATIONAL ORIGINS

The Peranakan and other similar local-born Chinese communities were built on the pre-national conditions under which early Chinese traders came to the region. I emphasize this pre-national feature because dynastic Ming and Qing China were sharply different from nationalist China of the twentieth century when the country set out to build a nation-state. Southeast Asia during the sixteenth to eighteenth century was also pre-national. Thus the Chinese traded and worked among peoples with different religions and cultures and responded to local conditions in different ways. They adjusted to the work and lifestyles of local populations and were widely accepted as valuable members of extensive trading networks. The Chinese who were born locally were enjoined to respect a few key elements of their faith and family practices, but would not have been expected to identify with the official sense of Chineseness associated with Ming and Qing China.[4] That was the first stage.

The growth of local-born communities prepared the foundations for the second stage, that is, when they accepted local linguistic usage. Languages at the time were also pre-national, in the sense that they observed no national borders. Eventually, one lingua franca prevailed in Nusantara or the Malay Archipelago, and that was Malay. It was functionally the lingua franca, and was to serve as the mother tongue for the young Chinese boys and girls who were born and brought up in the region. The language had no national connotation. It was used neither as a form of local Chinese patois, nor as a step towards identifying with the Malay peoples. Nevertheless, it was a conscious choice for the local-born to use Malay as the basis for their personal and communal communication. It became so effective that Peranakan writers emerged who developed considerable literary skills in it as well.[5] The two pre-national conditions above were central to the early formation of the Peranakan communities.

LIVING IN WESTERN NATIONAL EMPIRES

The third stage came when the communities were organized as subjects of what I call the new national empires. When the Dutch and the British East India Companies first came to Southeast Asia, they were mainly organized for commercial profit. Their leaders were aware that national interests were involved in the rivalry between their countries back home but they did not set out to build empires in Asia. But, in the course of the eighteenth century, there was a major political shift in Europe. This had begun from the late seventeenth century, when the idea of sovereign states began to emerge and some became more powerful than others. Most decisively, the Industrial Revolution in Britain made that country economically the most powerful in Western Europe. It was, however, the Dutch who qualify as the first modern nation-state when they freed themselves from the Spanish Netherlands to become the Dutch nation. As a republic of Dutch citizens, the country took steps to build a nation-state. So it was not surprising that eventually the East India Company was taken over by the Dutch state and the territories in the Malay world became the jewel in a Dutch national empire.

During the early years of the Industrial Revolution, it was the Dutch who had the keenest sense of being a nation. They had to fight off the Catholic Spanish empire on the one hand, and keep themselves distinct from their German and French neighbours on the other. Thus, as the Dutch developed a sense of their nationhood, the idea of nation-states based on language, religion and a common history spread among other European states.[6] Eventually, the most powerful were the two that built great national empires around the world, France and Britain. Because of the lead it had in the Industrial Revolution, Britain was to become the most powerful empire that the world had ever seen. The nation that manifested itself in France tried to be different and claimed to focus more on spreading civilization than on commerce. Indeed, powerful new ideas came out of the French Enlightenment that led to the French Revolution, and these did greatly enhance the concept of the glorious nation-state. That powerful mixture of enlightenment, idealism and nationalism made France the model for Europe for most of the nineteenth century. Nevertheless, British power, pioneering rapid industrial growth and maritime and naval supremacy, enabled the British to defeat everybody else at sea. What was more, it was the first time that the world was to see a nation-state that was at the core of a global national empire.

What was distinctive about this empire and made it unlike past empires is important. In the history books written in the West, it is normal to use the Roman Empire as the model by which other empires are compared for deviations and differences. The modern empire is totally new. Early theorists of imperialism, like Hobson and Lenin, have tied the origins of the British Empire to the rise of capitalism. Industrial capitalism was certainly one of the sources of the empire's power. But that ignores the cohesion and commitment that came from the nationals who won glory and control over lesser nations and thought it was their national superiority that made them the ruling elites of that empire. The Roman Empire and its successor feudal empires did not have that sense of national identity that came with the Dutch war of independence. The idea of nation was thereafter firmly integrated with state power, it was further uplifted after the new elites in Europe reacted to the ideas of revolutionary France, and was decisively confirmed by the naval might of Britain. After that, the idea of the glorious national empire was widely recognized as the best way for any country to become a Great Power.

Coming back to the Peranakan Chinese, it is no accident that they developed their distinctive identity in the territories ultimately dominated by these two powerful nation-states, the Dutch on the one hand, and the English on the other. That identity continued to be shaped by the governments that took over the failed East India companies at the end of the eighteenth and in the early nineteenth centuries. When that happened, the two trading empires were transformed into national empires in which national pride and dignity, the greatness of the nation, became tied up with the future of their imperial territories.

This concept of a national empire in which the Chinese and others came to be treated as their colonial subjects was evolved from the eighteenth century. It is significant that the Peranakan Chinese emerged as a distinct cluster of people with a designated relationship with the Dutch also in the eighteenth century. This was vividly underlined when thousands were identified as Chinese and massacred in Batavia in 1740. It was thus recognized that the Dutch were a nation as contrasted with native kingdoms that were also pre-national and not called nations, and there were other smaller native groups. Despite that tragic event, the Dutch still chose to treat Chinese as a valuable trading community.[7] It continued to be in Dutch interest to preserve that community and make them serve as semi- or sub-partners in their enterprise not only to help them to trade in the region but also, perhaps most of all, to trade with China.

In so doing, they provided the Chinese who worked closely with them a sense of identity that can be called proto-national. The Peranakan Chinese were probably not conscious of such an identity. That was not something that Chinese people saw of themselves. The empire under the Qing did not care about its Chinese subjects abroad at that time. Imperial policy was not concerned for those who were so foolish as to leave their country to live in some foreign land. Thus there was no official acknowledgement of there being any Chinese out in the Malay world. Most people in Qing China would not even have known of the existence of Chinese born abroad, least of all of their generations of descendants. In the simplest terms, Peranakan identity could only have been proto-national because, although Chinese communities organized themselves in distinct ways, China was a Manchu empire and not in the least national like the modern European nations.

FACING NATIONALISTIC CHINA

This leads me to the fourth stage, how the Peranakan Chinese became aware of their intermediate position when they faced the rise of a newly nationalistic China. It was difficult for them to come to terms with the pressure to be nationalistic Chinese in a changing political environment. They were proud to call themselves Chinese and many were ready to respond to the demands of a new China. But the criteria of who were true Chinese had been redefined. A new nation-state after the 1911 Revolution was proclaimed as the Republic of China. The Peranakan were aware that Sun Yat-sen and his followers had been spreading the idea of a Chinese nation amongst them in Malaya and the Netherlands East Indies. They knew that the idea attracted the attention of overseas Chinese everywhere. Nevertheless, for the Chinese in Southeast Asia, discovering this new urge for nationality, nationhood and nationalism was a new experience. For the Totok or genuine Chinese who had recently come from China, the simple idea of overthrowing the Manchu and restoring Han Chinese power was a particularly exciting experience. Theirs had been initially closer to a cultural identification with traditional China rather than to nationalist goals, but their newfound enthusiasm for the revolution nevertheless put pressure on members of the Peranakan community to follow suit.

This marked a major shift in the relationship between Peranakan and Totok (or *sinkheh*, newcomer) Chinese. The Peranakan throughout most of the nineteenth and early decades of the twentieth centuries were often in positions of privilege, and had assisted the Dutch or the British in local social and economic affairs. With that special relationship, they could at the same time help the Totok Chinese who came to work for them or do business with them. By providing a bridge between colonial governments and recent immigrants, their Peranakan status and identity was respected to greater or lesser extent on both sides. That had given the local-born a sense of being proto-national that the Chinese who had come directly from China did not have. Those new Chinese would have been aroused by Sun

Yat-sen's call for nationalism without having shared the earlier Peranakan experience of a having a proto-national position in other peoples' national empires. Thus, by the 1920s, there was increasing pressure on the Peranakan to become nationalistic Chinese. This was particularly so after the Guomindang seized power in 1928 and asked all *huaqiao* (overseas Chinese) to be patriotic. The governments in both Beijing and Nanjing of the early twentieth century had identified the Chinese abroad as *huaqiao*, and the Peranakan were labelled in a similar way. This pressure came in many forms and at many levels. Most notably, it came through Chinese education, in the numerous new schools that were founded to teach in Chinese, and the many Chinese newspapers that were published, as well as through the rapid growth of trading relationships between Nationalist China and British Malaya and the Netherlands East Indies.

After the 1850s, there were also far more Chinese coming out of China than before, particularly to the Straits Settlements and the Malay States. In proportion, the increase was less marked in the Netherlands East Indies, which is one of the reasons why the Chinese Peranakan remained in a stronger position there. In Malaya, Peranakan numbers diminished in relation to the newcomers. As a result, the pressure to conform to Chinese nationalism was even stronger in the Straits Settlements and the Malay States. Peranakan in elsewhere had more choices, given the changing relationship between themselves and the Dutch, between themselves and a new generation of Indonesian nationalists, and between themselves and Chinese officials and Totok Chinese. That was a triangular relationship whereby they had more space to manoeuvre than the recent arrivals had. The Peranakan's diminishing and marginalized position in the Straits Settlements and the Malay States made the community weaker during the 1930s.[8]

The Second World War marked an even more important change. When the Japanese took over in early 1942, being a Totok or a Peranakan was of no importance. The Peranakan had to face a new reality whether they liked it or not. As long as the Dutch or British were there, they could hold back from Chinese nationalism. There was room for them to stand up against pressures from official China if they wished to. But for three and a half years under the Japanese, there was no protection whatsoever. If and when the Japanese wanted to punish the Chinese, they did not ask whether someone was Peranakan or not. That was a traumatic and dramatic change to their particular identity as Peranakan.

DECOLONIZING SOUTHEAST ASIA

The fifth stage came with decolonization, when the Peranakan community was really divided and, I would add, often bewildered by what to do when the Dutch failed to regain control in Indonesia in 1945, and even when the British actually came back to Malaya and remained another twelve years. It was quite clear that the decolonization process was unstoppable and, where Malaya was concerned, it was only a matter of time before the British would leave. So it was a period of transition when the Peranakan had to re-examine where they stood. We know what were some of the choices and decisions that the Peranakan had to make in the nation-states of Indonesia and Malaysia. They varied from accepting a new nationality to realigning with the larger Chinese population, and to remigrating to other countries to seek a fresh start. The proto-national community was thereafter scattered and divided, unable to define a common course of action. This was totally understandable because other communities also found it difficult to adjust to the post-colonial situation. In general, most people recognized that indigenous nationalism had a right to shape and develop the former colonies into new nation-states.

In that context, there were some efforts to use the earlier proto-national identity of the Peranakan to re-establish an in-between position as a bridge between indigenous and immigrant nationalisms. It is interesting to see how Tan Cheng Lock played that role. I am not sure how deliberate he was about his role, or how far he was conscious of it. What happened was that both the Malay leadership and various groups of Chinese organizations found someone like him to be a valuable person to have. The new Malay nationalist government was closer to the British in the way they dealt with community leaders. They needed a group of Chinese to serve as a bridge between them and those whom they saw as more difficult to handle and ideologically threatening. Not many Peranakan could meet that need. But Tan Cheng Lock was exceptional because he not only tried but actually succeeded to provide the bridge that the two communities wanted, with the new Malay elites stepping into the shoes of the British to establish the new national authority. Tan Cheng Lock and his colleagues, some with Peranakan backgrounds, recognized and identified the new political role they needed to play, and the majority of the Chinese at that time accepted his leadership. They could see that he could talk to the Malay nationalist leadership in a way that most of them were unable to.

GOING GLOBAL: CHINA, CHINESE CULTURE AND THE PERANAKAN

This takes me to the sixth, the current, stage. Today, the Peranakan may look to transnational choices in order to avoid being marginalized by the new nation-states they live in. It is premature to speculate as to what will happen, so I shall simply pose a few questions here. Will the Peranakan be forced to accept a stronger kind of Chinese identity even though they may not be comfortable with that? Is there scope for them to seek some kind of post-national identity in which they do not have to be locally assimilated? In a transnational global environment, would there be greater scope anyway for them to play post-national roles, and find new space for themselves?

The Peranakan phenomenon has a peculiar place in the formation of the modern Chinese state. Its early appearance during the nineteenth century implicitly questioned the universality of the Chinese civilization, and even the relevance of national culture to those who identified primarily with the civilization. Can the concept of nationalistic Chinese culture coexist with transnational or post-national aspirations? Do we expect Chinese cultural values to appeal as before to Chinese all over the world no matter where they are? Is nationalism necessary for China? Should all Chinese be nationalistic? The existence of the Peranakan suggests that any answer to such questions should be closely examined. In this context, I shall go back to the recent past, adding some perspectives from the point of view of China, and raise four related points that may help us think about the future.

The Qing Dynasty

The most interesting to me is the first. This was when the Qing state discovered very late, during the second half of the nineteenth century, that there were Peranakan communities out there in Southeast Asia. When they sent their diplomatic officials to Singapore and elsewhere, they found Chinese communities that were well established under prosperous merchant leadership. They were surprised how the British and the Dutch seemed to trust them and seemed to rely on them to fulfill many of their commercial needs. The Qing image of the Chinese abroad as people likely to create trouble for China and the China coast was not borne out in the reports that these diplomats wrote home. On the contrary, these Chinese were proud to identify themselves as Chinese.

On discovering these Peranakan communities in the Nanyang, the response of the Qing mandarins was very interesting. On the one hand, they were quick to see an opportunity to use these prosperous and respected Chinese communities to help them deal with the British and other Europeans. On the other hand, they also noted that anti-Manchu sentiments could be found not far below the surface, including among the Peranakan. There had been millions of Han Chinese who were opposed to the Manchu conquerors of China since the end of the seventeenth century. That opposition was largely crushed and did not survive in most of China. But the sentiments survived in the Nanyang among the secret societies that had come from the provinces of Fujian and Guangdong. These two southern provinces had resisted the Manchu armies fiercely and many of those who left China for the Malay world were able to transmit some of that resentment to their descendants. Thus there were contradictory currents. Qing officials were glad to find Chinese out there who were rich and influential. They were fascinated by the fact that many of these prosperous Chinese were eager to be acknowledged by the Qing court and be treated as important.[9] The poorer newcomers who had recently come out of China, however, did not share that eagerness and remained hostile to Manchu dominance at home. The Peranakan were aware of the differences in attitude. Many of them were attracted by Qing official attention but, at the same time, they were also linked to local Chinese organizations that deeply resented the Manchus.

The Peranakan was a proto-national community in the colonial framework. They had experienced the nationalism of the Dutch and British and knew what it meant to be members of a great nation. Thus they could themselves respond to the nationalistic ideas that had begun to develop in their midst. It was, therefore, not surprising that when Sun Yat-sen turned up in Malaya, he was warmly received by some of them. But, Sun's main support came not so much from the rich and prosperous as from those who had recently arrived. These *sinkheh* included those who were aware of the unrest in southern China following the Taiping Rebellion, or had participated in the many revolts that were occurring throughout the empire, and they responded readily to the idea of driving out the Manchus.[10] The Peranakan were uncertain and ambivalent about that. Those who had a modern education and some sense of their proto-national identity were drawn to Sun Yat-Sen and his followers, and saw them as part of the modernization process that they themselves had gone through. They could empathize with that. At the same time, they retained their close relationships with the Dutch and the British, and were also wooed by officials of the Qing court, and that put many of them in an ambivalent position.

The idea of China among the Peranakan communities was also changing. Previously, they could focus on Chinese customs, festivals, rituals and practices that they had preserved to sustain their Chineseness. The China of the Qing state had nothing to do with that. But, with the turn towards modernization, there were new cutting edges to the idea of a Chinese nation. One of the sharper edges was to make people feel the sense of national pride. Thus the idea of China was being examined afresh and the Peranakan Chinese responded very differently. For example, there was Gu Hongming who went back to serve in Qing China and rejected nationalism and anti-Manchu sentiments absolutely. He even praised the Qing dynasty as representing the best features of Chinese civilization.[11] Then there was Lim Boon Keng a generation later, who was the most Confucian of all the Baba who have written about Chinese philosophy. He sympathized with Sun Yat-sen's revolutionary cause and returned to China to serve the new Xiamen University that his *sinkheh* friend, Tan Kah Kee, had founded.[12] Yet others expressed support for China's modernization in the areas of commerce and industry.

On the other hand, most of the *sinkheh* were keen to listen to Sun Yat-sen. Some of them later became so nationalistic that they even became hostile to the Peranakan. They thought the Peranakan were not Chinese enough and exhorted them to become more Chinese, not merely to demonstrate their nationalism but also to learn Chinese in order to better understand Chinese culture. There were different responses in different parts of the Nanyang. In the Netherlands East Indies, the Peranakan responses seemed also to have varied a lot and I find the differences interesting. I have not done enough research to draw any conclusions here but wish simply to draw attention to the range of responses to the traumatic events that confronted all kinds of Chinese at the end of the nineteenth century and early twentieth century.

The Republican Period

The second point arises from the fact that the new Chinese Republic after 1911 was very weak. During the first half of the twentieth century, several foreign powers took advantage of that weakness. The era of warlords and the Chinese civil war that lasted for over twenty years tempted the Japanese to invade the country, and demonstrated that the survival of China was at stake. In that context, the Peranakan Chinese can be said to have gained some time to consider their future. But, for the nationalistic *huaqiao*, the patriotic *aiguo huaqiao*, any hesitation on the part of the Peranakan to support China to the best of their ability added to doubts that they were really Chinese.

Chinese officials were uncertain how to handle the political cracks that emerged. While they insisted that every Chinese was a Chinese who was temporarily resident abroad, they also knew that this was not true. Tens of thousands of Peranakan were descended from generations of Chinese who did not see themselves as *huaqiao*. Official documents used gentle and polite language to overcome the ambiguities and but showed that they were aware of the actual position of many Peranakan leaders. The documents called them *huaqiao* while recognizing that they were Peranakan leaders of the different communities in British Malaya and the Dutch East Indies. The Chinese consular officials knew that most Peranakan were British or Dutch subjects and understood why the Peranakan were not as enthusiastic about national identity as the *sinkheh*. Thus Chinese officials were ambivalent about how to determine the place of the Peranakan and took great care to maintain good relations with these leaders.[13]

Because they were unable to define whom these Chinese were, they failed to appreciate the tensions that existed in the very nature of the Peranakan communities. These communities had struggled to hold on to their identity as Chinese over a very long time. They had then, for over a century, responded to the modernizing world around them, often keenly and creatively. Some of them had studied Western civilization and observed the course of global change while retaining a deep interest in Chinese culture and being conscious of their own distinctive sense of Chineseness. Thus their responses were not limited to commerce and privilege but included the acquisition of growing areas of modern knowledge and skills. But the Chinese revolutionary mood of the time demanded more than that and there was no patience for those who did not commit themselves to China's destiny. Despite that, however, the period was not one where the Peranakan leadership lost heart, but actually one of creativity during which many fought hard to sort out their heritage and their predicament. Among them were those who led Singapore to independence in 1965 and made the city-state a notable success story.

Peranakan and National History

The third point comes from the way the Peranakan were accepted into the new national histories of Malaysia, Singapore or Indonesia. This has some far-reaching effects. China learned that, although the Peranakan may have been the subjects of other states, they still saw themselves as culturally Chinese. And, even though they were increasingly marginal to Chinese national interests, that phenomenon did make some Chinese leaders aware of the possible nuances of multiple loyalties between official nationalities. These included hybrid cultural identities, something that the Chinese had not thought about before, which the persistence of Peranakan identity in other nations brought to the surface. Whether China liked it or not, this was a phenomenon that its legal and social institutions had to take into account. It ultimately helped Chinese leaders to think about some of the fuzzy edges of their own nation-state. To this day, as that state is still struggling to define itself, it has to be conscious of what is happening outside China.[14] There is now an increasing range of subtle identity differences that exist in the transnational world. Chinese awareness of that subtlety came when their officials first discovered the Nanyang Peranakan communities.

The Relevance of the Peranakan Phenomenon

The last point concerns a rising China. As China becomes more prosperous and powerful, is the Peranakan phenomenon more relevant or less? The Southeast Asian manifestation, although exceptional in many ways, has shown us how resilient it can be and suggests that this is a phenomenon that could grow to become more extended and various. When I spoke to the Peranakan Association, I suggested that such a development would hinge on not defining the Peranakan too narrowly. How the idea is defined is important. Professor Suryadinata has rightly argued that we need to know what we are talking about. If the term is defined narrowly, that is one thing. But if it is defined more widely to refer to local-born Chinese who remain Chinese after having interacted with many different cultures in complex ways, then such a phenomenon could be very significant in a transnational, globalized world. It is too early to say how significant it will be, but certainly so if it becomes a part of modern discourse, that is, not as something in the past, or something in the traditional museum that treats its artefacts as past and dead. As mentioned earlier, good museums do not do that. For example, the Peranakan Museum already symbolizes something that is encouraging and stimulating that can provoke new ways of thinking about the phenomenon.

In that context, Singapore could be a kind of crucible where the post-national form of Chineseness could become accepted by China. This is an interesting prospect. China approves of Singapore for many reasons. That may indicate a willingness to recognize a new kind of Peranakan Chinese community in Singapore, something that goes beyond the traditional Peranakan. I was intrigued when the Prime Minister, Mr Lee Hsien Loong, at the opening of the Peranakan Museum, said that he was a member of the community. The word is obviously no longer something to be shy about, something to be thought of as a cute and quaint label. It is still too early to speculate as to what this might mean in time to come. But it suggests that Singapore could be a place where post-national kinds of Chineseness could be accepted by

China. And that would in turn have an impact on other local-born Chinese around the world.

CONCLUDING REMARKS

A strong China would care more about its place in world politics than for the identities of ethnic minorities of Chinese descent who reside in states where China is looking for friends, or in states that want to be friendly with China. Under those conditions, external Chinese communities are likely to decide that they should shift back to stress their identification with culture. I think that trend has begun and that China will come to approve of it. The emphasis on cultural factors in contrast to the nationality factor in determining Chineseness is occurring. I do not know how far it will go, but it reminds us of the way culture played a central role in the pre-national and formative stage of the Peranakan communities. The contemporary shift could provide protection for new kinds of Peranakan to shape their identities around cultural artefacts, whether material or otherwise. In a world of extensive transnational communications, this phenomenon can only be seen as something forward-looking that opens up new areas of post-national identities.

Foreign nation-states whose citizens of Chinese origin are increasingly local born, and who find them useful to help build cooperative relations with China, might actually encourage some kind of cross-border identity. That would be familiar to the Peranakan for whom such a position had been the norm for centuries. But it would depend on China not being seen by its neighbours as threatening in any way. That is a major condition over which none of us have any control. In the end, China will recognize that it can afford to leave the ethnic Chinese alone to prosper abroad as foreign nationals and assume that these local born will feel something for China and understand Chinese interests and values. That will enable China and these varieties of ethnic Chinese to maintain an open and flexible attitude towards issues like nationality and political loyalty. And this would be even more so when China itself produces within its own borders people who are also more transnational in their outlook and share the professional and global skills that the foreign-born Chinese already have.

Under those conditions, some of the new communities could share the multiplicity of cultural artefacts that are increasingly borderless and even enjoy comfort zones when wearing their non-Chinese national identities on their sleeves. Most of all, they could rediscover an ability to mix their functional national languages with the Chinese language that they can now acquire if they want to. That would enhance their social and sub-official positions in their relationships with China. This will not make them quite like the Peranakan of Southeast Asian communities that thrived from the eighteenth to early twentieth centuries, but the new communities might still be recognized as new manifestations of what I call the Peranakan phenomenon.

Notes

1. It is perhaps not coincidental that Dr Goh Keng Swee's mother was a cousin of Tun Tan Cheng Lock. Tan Cheng Lock's place in history may be discerned in two recent essays: Kwa Chong Guan, "The political dilemmas and transformation of the straits-born Chinese community, the era of decolonization"; and Lee Kam Hing, "Peranakan Chinese community and decolonization in Malaya", in *Peranakan Communities in the Era of Decolonization and Globalization*, edited by Leo Suryadinata (Singapore: Chinese Heritage Centre and NUS Baba House, 2014).
2. Introduction to Leo Suryadinata, ed., *Peranakan Chinese*. The fullest

and most important study of the Babas of Malacca and Singapore are Tan Chee Beng, *The Baba of Malacca: Culture and identity of a Chinese Peranakan community in Malaysia* (Petaling Jaya: Pelanduk Publications, 1988); and Jurgen Rudolph, *Reconstructing Identities: A social history of the Babas in Singapore* (Aldershot: Ashgate Publishing, 1998). On the role of the Nyonya matriarch, Gwee Thian Hock, *A Nyonya mosaic: My mother's childhood* (Singapore: Times International, 1985) and Queeny Chang, *Memoirs of a Nonya* (Singapore: Eastern University Press, 1981).

I also refer to the particular significance of the Nyonya's role in my "Foreword" to Ong Chwee Lim, comp., *Chew Boon Lay: A family traces its history* (Singapore: privately published, 2003).

3. Introduction to Leonard Blussé and Chen Menghong, eds., *The archives of the Kong Koan of Batavia* (Leiden: Brill, 2003).

4. How the identity evolved by the eighteenth century may be seen in the discussions on the Hokkien communities, James K. Chin, "Merchants and other sojourners: the Hokkiens overseas, 1570–1760", PhD Thesis, University of Hong Kong, 1998.

5. This stage of change is introduced by Claudine Salmon and Denys Lombard in *The Chinese of Jakarta: Temples and communal life* (Archipel: Etudes Insulindiennes 1, Societe pour l'Etude et la Connaissance du Monde Insulindiennes. Paris: Editons de la Maison des sciences de l'homme, 1980); and further developed in Claudine Salmon, *Literary Migrations: Traditional Chinese fiction in Asia (17–20th centuries)* (Beijing: International Culture Publishers, 1987; reprinted in Singapore: Institute of Southeast Asian Studies, 2013).

6. I shall not get into the debate about the medieval origins of modern nations. The numerous studies of the beginnings of nation building favour the end of the eighteenth century, Guntram H. Herb and David H Kaplan, eds, *Nations and Nationalism: A Global Historical Overview*, Vol. 1 (1770–1880), (Santa Barbara: ABC-CLIO, 2008). Adrian Hastings is persuasive in stressing the Christian origins of the nation idea and, as can be seen in the two decades of articles on the subject in the journal *Nations and Nationalism*, it is clear much

depends on how nation is defined. The evidence for the modern nation-state beginning with the success of the Dutch revolt against imperial Spain seems to me convincing, Jonathan Israel, *The Dutch republic: Its rise, greatness, and fall, 1477–1806* (Oxford: Oxford University Press, 1995).

7. J. Th Vermuelen, *De Chineezen te Batavia en de troebelen van 1740* (Leiden: 1938), translated into English as "The Chinese in Batavia and the troubles of 1740", by Tan Yeok Seong, in 《南洋学报》 (*Journal of the South Seas Society*) 9, no. 1 (1953), reprinted in 陈育崧, 《椰阴馆文存》 [Collected essays of Yeyinguan], 新加坡: 南洋学会 (1983), vol. 3.

8. Yen Ching-huang, *The overseas Chinese and the 1911 Revolution, with special reference to Singapore and Malaya* (Kuala Lumpur: Oxford University Press, East Asian historical monographs series, 1976); Yong (C.F.) Ching Fatt, *Chinese leadership and power in colonial Singapore* (Singapore: Times Academic Press, 1992). Also, Png Poh Seng, "The Straits Chinese in Singapore: a case of local identity and socio-cultural accommodation", *Journal of Southeast Asian History* 10, no. 1 (1969).

9. 黄遵宪 (Huang Zunxian), "番客" (Foreigner), a poem reproduced in 柯木林、林孝胜著 《新华历史与人物研究》 [Study of personalities in Singapore history], 南洋学会, 1986. Wen, Chung Chi, "The nineteenth-century Imperial Chinese Consulate in the Straits Settlements: origins and development", unpublished MA Thesis, Department of History, University of Singapore, 1964.

10. 张永福 《南洋与创立民国》 [Nanyang and the establishment of the Chinese Republic] (上海: 上海中华書局, 1933). Republished in 2013 by 新加坡: 晚晴园 – 孙中山南洋纪念馆出版社, 2013.

11. My Tsai lecture at Harvard, "Tianxia: Perspectives from outside of China", in *Renewal: The Chinese State and the New Global History* (Hong Kong: The Chinese University Press, 2013).

12. Lim Boon Keng's numerous articles in *The Straits Chinese Magazine* have been collected; *Essays of Lim Boon Keng on Confucianism*, with Chinese translations by Yan Chunbao (Singapore: World Scientific Publishing e-Book, 2015). His conflict with the modernists of his

time was brought out most sharply when Lu Xun openly criticized him, Wang Gungwu, "Lu Xun, Lim Boon Keng and Confucianism", *Papers on Far Eastern History*, no. 39 (Canberra, 1989); also in *China and the Chinese Overseas* (Singapore: Times Academic Press, 1991). Translated into Chinese, "鲁迅、林文庆和儒家思想" in 《中国与海外华人》(香港: 商务印书馆, 1994).

13. C.F. Yong and R.B. McKenna, *The Kuomintang movement in British Malaya, 1912–1949* (Singapore: Singapore University Press , c.1990).

14. The current debate within China about "What is China?" reflects increased sensitivity about nationals and citizens who are only marginally Chinese, or even deny that they are Chinese. Much of the writing since 2014 has been collected in over 200 issues of an internally circulated set of papers, 民族社会学研究通讯 at Peking University. Also 马戎 (Ma Rong) 编著 《民族社会学: 社会学的族群关系研究》[Sociology of Ethnic Studies] (北京: 北京大學出版社, 2004). Key historians engaged in the debate include Ge Zhaoguang 葛兆光, whose book 《宅兹中国: 重建有關中国的歷史論述》[Home in China: Rebuilding the historical discourse on Zhongguo] (台北市: 聯經出版事業股份有限公司, 2011), galvanized some of the debates.

Chapter 6

SINGAPORE, LOYALTY AND IDENTITY

In Song Ong Siang's *One Hundred Years' History of the Chinese in Singapore*, the ambiguity of identity in the nineteenth century Baba (now more commonly called Peranakan) or Straits Chinese community as compared with the finely differentiated and multiple labels used by the newcomers from China was striking.[1] But, as far as I can tell, both groups of Chinese experienced uncertainty when it came to more modern ideas of loyalty. There were questions like, how should they show loyalty to an emerging sense of nation in China as compared with local British authority? Which had priority? Could they put their cultural heritage, customs and practices and family priorities above the

This is a slightly revised version of a lecture on "Chinese identity and loyalty in Singapore in the 19th and 20th centuries". It is part of the National Library Prominent Speaker Series and was given at The Pod in the National Library on 26 July 2016. Extracts from it were published online in mothership.sg on 28 May 2017. The Chinese translation was published in 《华人研究国际学报》 [The International Journal of Diasporic Chinese Studies] in 2017, pp. 1–12.

calls to support race-and-nation salvation? What should they do when different parties fighting for power in Republican China asked for their allegiance?

When I was invited to talk about identity and loyalty in Singapore, I knew that the National Library did not expect a lecture to do justice to a topic that would need volumes to cover. They wanted to draw attention to it and have someone open up a discussion on how it might be perceived today. I am content to do just that. For decades, I have struggled off and on with aspects of Chinese identity in China and among Chinese overseas.[2] In 1985, I went beyond the safety of history to explore recent perspectives and hosted a conference at the Australian National University on "Changing identities of the Southeast Asian Chinese since World War II". That made me even more aware how difficult it is to pin down the concept of identity in a world that was changing fast during the twentieth century.[3]

Here I shall share with you some of my ideas about identity. It is foolhardy of me to do this in front of an audience of Singaporeans. I am conscious that I am not telling you anything new about this city-state but hope that you will find it interesting to hear my efforts to understand the subject. What is new for me is to try and connect identity with loyalty. I believe that identity precedes loyalty. It can clarify what one is to be loyal to. This is an issue I have taken for granted and not carefully examined before. I have found thinking about it for this lecture has helped me clear up some uncertainties in my mind.

It is well known that there has never been only one kind of Chinese identity. This is particularly true of those who left home to settle abroad and had to adapt to different circumstances and social and political environments. Like migrants everywhere, Chinese have multiple identities, some superficial and momentary, others deep and permanent.

At the personal level, Chinese can choose which identity to emphasize at any one time. That could come from a wide range, from surface identities linked with work, hobby, and social circles to deep and passionate ones expressed through commitments to family, country, religious faith, even a political party and its ideology. Also, different adjectives might be used to characterize their identity, for example, arrogant, cunning, hardworking, backward, superstitious, China-centred. With each of them, various cultural and political judgments were made. For centuries, most Chinese were powerless to change such labelling by others and were frustrated by their failure to prove them misleading or wrong.

Obviously, self-identity as Chinese could be quite different from being identified by others as someone who is Chinese. Often, attributes are selectively used — such as filial son, loyal brother, friend or partner — to describe what was Chinese. These could be used to determine how Chinese someone was. Also, when we speak of different kinds of Chinese, we might expect them to have different identity mixes, for example, those found among Baba or *sinkheh*, traditionalists or radicals, Chinese-educated or English-educated. We would expect these mixes to emphasize different identities to different peoples, at different times and places. Certainly, there are official and legal identities that cannot be freely challenged, for example, being registered as Chinese when at point of entry to Singapore or in a court of law, or when receiving travel papers, and permits to set up businesses.

Most people thus have more than one identity and are unlikely to have a single unchanging identity all their lives. How then does identity relate to loyalty? We can speak of degrees of loyalty as we can of layers of identity. For example, traditional Chinese placed loyalty to family above all others and that could translate to loyalty to the chief, the prince, the emperor, and all forms of authority. But they also recognized loyalty to friends and partners in any enterprise and often used kinship terms to describe that. Today, Chinese like many others may expect loyalty to country to take precedence, even to the extent of saying, my country right or wrong.

But others would claim that there are loyalties that rise above that. The strongest are values conscientiously expressed that are akin to absolutes in religious faith, followed by assertions of right and wrong. But also where there are clear injunctions to perform certain rites at specific times, for example, practices in relation to births and deaths, to rites of passage and marriage conditions. These must be respected and may override all other loyalties.

Unlike identity, conflicts of loyalty can be more unyielding. In the two centuries of Singapore's modern history, some kinds of loyalty have coexisted like being a British subject and culturally Chinese. Others, like being loyal to a family and to a god or a set of gods, and to a secret society or a banned political party. What prevailed was often determined by the exercise of force and law. Most of the time, however, the practices of a plural society allowed some give and take and the freedom to choose. This is the background to the expressions of identity and loyalty in three distinct periods in modern Singapore history.

The first period takes us from the early years to the 1870s when the port colony came to be seen as the centre of a larger polity under British administration and control.

The second is when British Malaya emerged as a mixed form of colonial state, and rising Chinese collective interests sought to redefine their place in it. Later, these interests led some Chinese to prepare for new roles once they saw that the British would eventually depart.

The third follows the changes during the past fifty years when the new regime was challenged to convince a Chinese

majority population that it was in their best interests to lead
a plural society to become a kind of nation-state. Beyond that,
they could also help to propel Singapore to an important place
in the global economy.

EARLY SINGAPORE

For a few decades, Singapore was the newest port in the Malay
world. The first Chinese who came from that world were
largely Baba Chinese who had worked with Dutch and British
merchants keenly interested in trading with China. They came
largely from Malacca and the nearby islands, and were familiar
with the Malay elites as well as with Anglo-Dutch officials. The
British found them invaluable to get the port off to a good
start. Most of them were descendants of Chinese men with local
wives. They were a closely-knit group proud of their ancestral
customs and practices but did not identify with their homes
in China. Others had also been trading and working in the
neighbourhood and received help from Baba Chinese to work in
Singapore. Theirs was a *xiangtu* (native or local) culture brought
out of their homes in China. They knew their family and village
origins and located them in entities like Fujian and Guangdong
but did not identify with the Qing Empire. If anything, they
sympathized with those who hated the Manchus and wanted
to restore Han Chinese rule.[4]

After the British took Hong Kong and opened up Treaty Ports
in China, many more Chinese spread out to different continents,
including thousands who came to Singapore on the way to other
islands and the Malay States. Many of them stayed on, and they
soon outnumbered the earlier Baba Chinese. The British had
to learn to differentiate between the varieties of peoples who
stressed their different origins and were organized accordingly.

The Babas were counted on to be relatively loyal to colonial rule, while the *sinkheh* newcomers were only loyal to their kinsmen. Some were active in the secret "brotherhoods" that defended and fought for them.

It was also a time when the imperial order in China faced numerous rebellions. The most serious of these, the Taiping Heavenly Kingdom, was exceptionally brutal not only against Manchu rule but also against the literati classes. These rebels upended all traditional norms. When they finally failed, many survivors escaped to the Malay world, including to Singapore. They identified with the secret societies and were usually alienated from any established authority. Although small in number, they were activist and tended to identify with clandestine organizations.

The Chinese quickly became the majority population in Singapore. The British took special measures to ensure that their rival organizations avoided open conflict and respected British laws. A new kind of identity was introduced to the Singapore-born. When any of them traded in China's treaty ports, British consular services protected them as British subjects. Qing officials resented this and some began to rethink their policy towards the Chinese overseas. However, it was not until the 1870s that policies were changed and the first consuls were appointed to Singapore. The officials discovered that the well-established Chinese welcomed their offers of protection as subjects of the Qing Empire. Thus some could become two kinds of imperial subjects, British and Chinese.

Most Chinese were proud to be Chinese whatever that meant to the British and Dutch and various Malay and Thai rulers. But the idea of being Chinese "nationals" did not yet arise. Other loyalties prevailed, from filial piety to parents and loyalty to immediate family, to inherited religious practices and other cultural artifacts, and, collectively, to their district or dialect communities. They had no expectations from Qing China. Instead, where the British provided effective governance, some Chinese enjoyed special relations with colonial authority. Thus, the Chinese lived with multiple identities and chose which ones to stress when called for. At the same time, there was a hierarchy of loyalties where family would come first, but allegiances to whoever could help their livelihood were allowed.

BRITISH MALAYA AND CHINESE NATION

The 1870s marked a turning point. For the British, intervention in the Malay States following the Treaty of Pangkor created new regimes of control. For the Chinese, the new consulate-general in Singapore was the first step in giving them an officially recognized identity. More Chinese were now drawn to British Malaya and many of them used Singapore as their base. The establishment of a consulate was a reminder that this was a time when the idea that everyone should belong to some nation or another was spreading around the world. Thus the Chinese overseas, whether China-born or British subjects, were seen as citizens or nationals temporarily living abroad, hence the idea of being *huaqiao*. In that capacity, these Chinese found it increasingly painful to see Qing China continue to weaken, and its efforts to modernize and reform being aborted. Some Chinese then openly supported the drive to reject the Manchu as foreign rulers. That gave them a baseline for a growing *national* awareness. Being Chinese was redefined by using terms that were barely distinguishable from those that Japan had adopted from European nation-states in order to unite its people.

The pre-national Malay world around Singapore was similarly aroused. What being Chinese meant was now questioned at all levels of society, not least by those who saw them as foreign immigrants. At one end, everyone who originated from China was grouped together as Chinese. This implied a single collective of people. Sun Yat-sen, who had lived among the Chinese in Singapore and Penang and wanted unity among them, was unimpressed. He compared the Chinese to a large plate of loose sand, unable to cooperate and difficult to unite.

At the other end, Straits Chinese who claimed to be loyal to the British Empire contributed money and effort to support Empire war efforts from the Boer War to two World Wars. In between were men with Baba background like Gu Hongming who discarded what he was taught about modern Western civilization and passionately supported the total retention of Confucian traditional values. Others like Lim Boon Keng moved only half-way and wanted Chinese to be both modern and Confucian.[5] Yet others were more decisive. Tan Kah Kee aligned his Hokkien culture with national aspirations and exhorted his compatriots to identify fully with the new China. He was clear what being Chinese meant and was steadfast in acting as a patriot.[6]

But uncertainty remained about what defined a Chinese. After the fall of the Manchu, a new formula was devised to include everyone within the borders of the former Qing Empire. The "Five-nation republic" (*wuzu gonghe*, 五族共和) identified the Han, Manchu, Mongol, Muslim Hui and Tibetan peoples as Chinese, as *zhonghuaminzu* 中华民族. This new inclusive definition meant that China was nation building on a different platform. For those in Singapore who came from southern China, this new construct was abstract and remote. So the Chinese republic launched a massive campaign to re-educate everyone to understand the new formula. The central theme was that the sacred land of China was being cut up and the country dismembered. Including everyone within the borders was the only way to defend the heritage. Being Chinese was thus raised to a much higher level.

Colonial policy encouraged Chinese to bring their families and settle but left them to educate their children. Modern schools sprouted quickly and adopted the Chinese national curriculum. New generations of teachers inspired by the May Fourth Movement brought their belief that Western scientific and democratic values could be used to unite China and recover its ancient glory. Newspapers educated the adult population to the power struggles all over China by bringing their politics into Singapore. Chinese of all classes began to shape their identities and loyalties in response.

The British were alarmed and tried to curb excessive nationalist displays. But the alternative of being Straits Chinese British subjects promised too little for those Chinese who were now politically aroused.[7] The Baba were divided. Some began to learn *guoyu*, the national language, and studied things Chinese to affirm their Chinese origins. National identity was widely asserted when the nationalists came to power in 1928. And when Japanese imperialists created the puppet state of Manchuria and pushed further inland into northern China, the rising tide of nationalism became overwhelming.

Japanese victories in Southeast Asia and the British surrender of Singapore hit the Chinese hardest. Three years of Japanese occupation forced them to rethink who they were. They reflected on their future beyond the British Empire. It was but a short step from anti-Japanese imperialism to anti-imperialism in general. Most people could now see a post-imperial world of independent states. This placed national identity above all others. The former colonies were ready to start afresh without Europeans in charge. Among Chinese, the numbers of local-born had caught up with those born in China. They looked for new identities and asked what they should now be loyal to. Could they be loyal to a new country and still retain a Chinese identity?

For the Singapore economy to recover after the war, law and order was necessary. For the poorer working classes, many were convinced that the time for exploitation was over. The fight for social justice was greatly appealing.[8] For the young, many more schools were built to prepare them as post-colonial nationals. They began to understand that the polity that replaced British rule would consist of a mix of peoples that looked to different national identities elsewhere, to China and India and to Indonesia-Melayu Raya.

After the war ended, people in Singapore asked what they could now be. Never before was it so urgent to find an answer. Never before had political identity been defined in narrow national terms. They also had to confront the failed vision of the Malayan Union. If Singapore were to be included in a communal-dominated Federation of Malaya, there would be further uncertainty.

On top of the layers of ethnic, social and cultural loyalties that everyone faced, the political identity of this Malaya was the central question. Should that state be in the hands of feudal bureaucrats and business classes carrying on the colonial heritage? Should it be a welfare state as many progressive states had become? Or one that chose the revolutionary path as in China, Vietnam and Indonesia? Or should it be a state where ethnic majority dominance determined all issues of identity and loyalty?

These processes could not be separated from the larger struggle for global dominance between the United States and the Soviet Union. Their Cold War had reached out to China and Southeast Asia. Once the Chinese Communist Party (CCP) won power on the mainland, no Chinese anywhere was immune to the pressure to identify with one side or the other. Political identity, whether based on ideology or ethnicity, began to overwhelm all others.

NATION-STATE, GLOBAL CITY

The decades of uncertainty in China and British Malaya from the late nineteenth century to the 1960s saw the challenge of many identities for the Chinese. Singapore was the centre for trade, news and education and became a node for change. Numerous teachers and journalists kept its Chinese population close to developments in China. Many official delegations visited Singapore regularly as well as hundreds of political exiles from the KMT-CCP civil war from 1928 to 1937. Furthermore, major efforts to raise funds to support the defence of China against the Japanese were inspired by community leaders like Tan Kah Kee. It is now hard to imagine how powerful the pull of China was for most Chinese in Singapore.

Even before the Japanese occupation, patriotism had become mainstream and it challenged any residual loyalty to the British and their idea of a pluralist port-city. Every Chinese could see that nationalism had become the most visible and potent political creed. Although many remained firm in their primary concern for family, clan and district associations, the pressure to give priority to national and ideological loyalties continued to grow. This was particularly true for the graduates of Chinese high schools. In comparison, many at English schools tended to identify with modern civic ideals from Britain or specific Christian values, and only few admired the national and revolutionary movements in China. It was clear that the products of the two education streams were growing apart. The war with Japan narrowed the gap for a while when Chinese and British interests coincided in their hatred of Japanese militarism. When the war ended, this was set aside when most of the Chinese-educated sympathized with the anti-colonial forces and wanted to see the British leave as soon as possible.

The Chinese remained divided into the 1950s. A small number continued to identify with the politics of China. A larger number engaged in the battle to determine their future in Singapore. But an even larger proportion longed for the return of normalcy so that they could protect their businesses and their livelihood. For this last group, the old formula of loyalty to family and local cultures remained paramount. They understood that Singapore was not China and could not ever claim to be part of China. They were content to live and work in a plural society and were ready to go on doing so. In that way, their cultural identity could be preserved and their children could share their loyalty to what they valued as intrinsically Chinese. As they saw it, what was central was continued access to the Chinese language. This was not only for practical reasons but also because it gave meaning to their moral and social life.

It was in this context that the campaign for Nanyang University was launched. Once it was clear that high school graduates could no longer pursue their tertiary education in China, the answer was obvious. Singapore should lead the way to build a Chinese-language university. The response not only in Malaya but also elsewhere in the region was overwhelming. Singapore Chinese once again had a central role in the Nanyang and a new kind of transnational Chinese could see it as their base. The British were not prepared to support this in its colony and non-Chinese political leaders shared their concerns. Some feared that Taiwan leaders would use it to nurture and recruit future anti-communist nationalists; others saw it as a potential seedbed to further radicalize high school graduates who already leant towards the new China.

But the desire to raise the language and cultural levels higher was deep and genuine. The new university was a beacon of light that could serve the Nanyang Chinese, a valuable asset to Singapore and, ultimately, to the Malaya it would one day be part of. Indeed, the founders had that cultural goal in mind. But the anti-communist war in Malaya with its anti-Chinese core, the "Ganyang Malaysia" campaign in Sukarno's Indonesia, and also the bitter battles that led to separation and independence for Singapore, all conspired to focus attention on the university's problems and not on its promise. Its political roles were consequently raised above its educational ideals.[9] Thus, instead of becoming an institution that the Chinese-educated could be loyal to, it stumbled along until forced to merge with the University of Singapore. That left a cultural vacuum that has only been partially mended.

In short, mainstream Chinese identity in Singapore was based on a language identity and loyalty, not on patriotism or chauvinism or the wish to import communism. Nor did it depend on any desire to restore traditional cultures. By the 1960s, after years of adapting to changing realities, that identity was committed to progress, to science, to freedom and democracy, to respect of the law, to whatever would enhance the lives of their families in the future Singapore. However, it failed to convince those who believed that Singapore's future had to be built on its plural society, those who from the start were afraid that this Chinese project would weaken if not undermine the multicultural foundations of the country.

After Singapore's independence, the goal of achieving a national identity was clear. Its people would focus on the nation as the object of prime loyalty. What distinguished the state was its small size with almost no natural resources, and its large Chinese population. The long and contested decolonization process after 1945 revealed how much existing national and ethnic identities could threaten the pluralist ideal. The different loyalties represented were strong and could not be ignored. Fortunately, most of the younger generation of Chinese educated after the war had decided that Singapore was their home. Their Chinese identity was not tied to either the mainland PRC or the ROC in Taiwan but was increasingly focused on their cultural heritage. The tumultuous events in China under Mao Zedong merely deepened the distance they now felt and, except among a few, being Chinese had nothing to do with communist ideology.

Other uncertainties remained, not least those brought by unfriendly elements among Singapore's neighbours. In that context, the failed September 30 coup in Indonesia only weeks after Singapore's independence was a stroke of good fortune. When the backlash against the coup destroyed the PKI (Communist Party of Indonesia), that was a great relief for the new state. Furthermore, the Cultural Revolution in China followed and the horrendous damage it did for Chinese culture and values removed any remaining inclination to admire that China. Singapore Chinese could now think afresh about the make-up of their country and reflect on the kind of identity and loyalty that could come out of a commitment to a pluralist state.

Everyone knew that this goal would not be easy to achieve. To define such a national identity that is not found anywhere else in Asia required careful and sensitive education for all concerned. The fact that power was in the hands of the Chinese majority made it incumbent on the leadership to ensure that this power was not used to undermine that pluralist ideal. It could not depend on force alone. In the long run, it hinged on building a deep understanding of the equal rights of all Singapore citizens and the guarantee of security among its minorities. Such commitment demanded open minds, a willingness to compromise, as well as great persuasive skill. Political parties are naturally tempted to woo voters by appealing to identity politics. It is therefore remarkable how that temptation has been curbed during the past fifty years.

Nevertheless, defining an identity acceptable to the majority Chinese population was not enough. The new republic needed to build a viable economy in which Chinese entrepreneurs would become major stakeholders who are able to create new jobs. Its history pointed to the port city's extended networks that served the region and beyond. Chinese businesses were in the best position to help the country become indispensable for transnational companies that wanted a hub in Southeast Asia. That also required peace in the workforce. The governing party knew that getting employers and employees to cooperate and share a common goal would dampen the appeal of identity politics among the working classes. It was significant how readily Chinese labour leaders responded to that development.

The idea of becoming a global city was farseeing. But the new state had to act cautiously at an early stage of its own nationhood. Depending on multinational corporations could inhibit the growth of a strong national identity. It could also affect the language-based identity most Chinese valued.[10] Fortunately, the rapid rise of China enabled Singapore to use that identity to its advantage. Second language learning was strongly supported by technological and financial skills. Most parents saw the benefits of that China connection and readily responded. The result was the drive to excel at all levels. It shows how this policy has done more for Singaporean Chinese identity than the political rhetoric used in the past. The majority community can now see its fear of cultural loss greatly reduced.

SINGAPORE CHINESE

I have not been asked to go beyond the twentieth century, so I shall not go further. But conditions are changing as the world adjusts to Chinese economic power. It is timely to ask how

Chinese cultural identity will change and how that will align with Singapore's national identity. How will the younger generation here respond to new identities in China? If their identity in Singapore were culturally secure, I would expect primary loyalty to Singapore not to be affected.

We have seen what the Chinese overseas in Singapore and elsewhere have been through since the nineteenth century. They have had to change parts of their identities several times and have learnt to manage the changes successfully. From the extreme demands of Chinese nationalism to accusations of being the fifth column of the communist world, from being called *hanjian* 汉奸 (traitors) by other Chinese to being labelled as alien (*pendatang*) by local *bumiputra*, they have been through it all. A deep-rooted pragmatism prevailed as they firmly confronted each kind of crisis and found themselves wiser and enriched by their experiences.

I began by saying that there has never been any one Chinese identity, that everyone has multiple identities. Chinese in Singapore were no exceptions. Over time, they learnt that Chinese were always diverse and it was in their own interest to acknowledge that diversity. That made most of them accept the norms of plural societies as something they could live with and benefit from.

I also suggested that each identity might call for a different level of loyalty: some are immediate and conditional while others are deep and unshakeable. And there could be a hierarchy of loyalties whereby some would always override the others, for example, when loyalty to family, country and culture are prioritized above all else.

Having outlined these developments, I am particularly impressed by the way Singapore Chinese responded to an exceptional situation. I refer to the years after 1965 when they found themselves as the majority population in their own state with their leaders democratically elected to take power. This was unknown for any Chinese community outside China, and there were no roadmaps to tell them what they should do. Their leaders fell back on what distinguished the port city of Singapore, the conditions that made them appreciate their lives in a plural society.[11] They had lived with that long enough to understand what that meant and therefore focused on what needed to be done to sustain it. Chinese leaders were wise enough not to abuse their majority position. Instead, they worked to find ways to create a new composite Singapore identity that would serve the country's long-term interests.

This is still work in progress. There will be further challenges to test what they have established. Future generations will always have to manage this enterprise with sensitivity and care. My tentative conclusion is that, given how the various Chinese in Singapore have been rational in dealing with multiple identities, they know how to distinguish the degrees of loyalty that these identities require.

The second half of the twentieth century saw the emergence of new norms for national identity. These expect the people of Singapore, not least the majority Chinese, to construct something beyond having multiple identities and exercising a hierarchy of loyalties. The ingredients for producing a composite identity are now present, although it is yet to have an agreed name. Such a construct would be contrary to ethnic-based national norms and would always need to be defended when challenged. But, given the possibility of building a pluralist nation that can also serve as a global city, I can imagine the Chinese communities, together with the others, contributing their share to that composite identity. What parts of the many identities in Singapore will that contain I do not know. What layers of loyalty that might evoke I also cannot foresee. However, I expect it to be an identity that is integrative and distinctively multidimensional. And Chinese experiences in Singapore will have a unique place in that condition, and that will allow Singaporeans to say that they are also Chinese.

Notes

1. A very useful annotated edition of Song Ong Siang's book, *One Hundred Years' History of the Chinese Singapore*, an annotated edition, is now available online. It is edited by Kevin Y.L. Tan, assisted by G. Uma Devi and Kua Bak Lim (Singapore Heritage Society), and published by the National Library Board, 2016. Linking that past with the rest of the twentieth century is *Great Peranakans: Fifty remarkable lives* (Singapore: Asian Civilisations Museum, 2015).

    There are other excellent examples of the multiple and colourful connections with the Baba Peranakan of the Malay world, for example, Khoo Joo Ee, *The Straits Chinese: A cultural history* (Amsterdam and Kuala Lumpur: The Pepin Press, 1996); Ronald G. Knapp, *Chinese Houses of Southeast Asia: The Eclectic Architecture of Sojourners and Settlers* (Tokyo: Tuttle Publishing, 2010); and Chan Suan Choo, *The Pinang Peranakan Mansion* (George Town, 2011).

2. I first began questioning the notion of Nanyang Chinese identity in eight radio talks for Radio Sarawak in 1958. That was when many writers in China and abroad still resisted the idea that not all Chinese overseas were *huaqiao* (Chinese temporarily living abroad). The talks were published as *A Short History of the Nanyang Chinese* (Singapore: Donald Moore, 1959). The book has been translated into Chinese and Japanese.

3. "The Study of Chinese Identities in Southeast Asia", in *Changing Identities of Southeast Asian Chinese since World War II*, co-edited with Jennifer Cushman (Hong Kong: Hong Kong University Press, 1988), pp. 1–21. Five of the essays in that volume discussed how the issue affected Singapore. Since then, research and analyses on the meaning of identity have been growing. I shall only mention

the collection of essays in Derek Heng and Syed Muhd Khairuddin Aljunied, eds, *Reframing Singapore: Memory — Identity — Trans-regionalism* (Amsterdam: Amsterdam University Press, 2009), notably its excellent bibliography.

4. Of particular interest are the research findings of Zhuang Qinyong (庄钦永) in 《新加坡华人与论丛》 [Essays on the Chinese in Singapore], published by 南洋学会 [South Seas Society], in 1986 and 《实叻峨嘈五虎祠义士新义》 [Heroic images of the Ming royalists: A re-examination of the spirit tablets previously housed at the five tigers shrine, Singapore] published in 1996. The literature concerning some early forms of loyalty beyond family and locality is summed up in Leon Comber, *Chinese secret societies in Malaya: A survey of the Triad Society from 1800 to 1900* (New York: J.J. Augustin for the Association for Asian Studies, 1959). Also relevant is the analysis of Chinese rivalries based on various kinds of loyalty in Lee Poh Ping, *Chinese society in 19th century Singapore* (Kuala Lumpur: Oxford University Press, 1978).

5. When Song Ong Siang and Lim Boon Keng started *The Straits Chinese Magazine: A Quarterly Journal of Oriental and Occidental Culture* in 1897, it was one kind of response to the rapid changes taking place in Anglo-Chinese relations and their impact on both identity and loyalty. When it ended in 1907, it was also because the position for both the British and the Chinese had changed. In particular, following the visits to Singapore of Kang Youwei and Sun Yat-sen at the turn of the century, attention had shifted to local battles about the fate of China; Yen Ching-hwang's several studies illuminate this transitional period well, beginning with *The Chinese and the 1911 Revolution, with special reference to Singapore and Malaya* (Kuala Lumpur: Oxford University Press, 1976). Offering direct comparisons of the three kinds of Chinese seeking to redefine themselves during this period of change is 李元瑾 (Lee Guan Kin), 《东西文化的撞击与新华知识分子的三种回应: 邱菽园, 林文庆, 宋旺相的比较研究》 [The clash of East and West: Three kinds of intellectual responses in Singapore: a comparative study of Khoo Seok Wan, Lim Boon Keng and Song Ong Siang] (新加坡: 新加坡国立大学中文系 [Chinese Studies Department, National University of Singapore], 2001), comparing the

responses to change of three contemporary thinkers, Qiu Shuyuan, Lin Wenqing and Song Wangxiang.

6. C.F. (Ching Fatt) Yong, *Chinese Leadership and Power in Colonial Singapore* (Singapore: Times Academic Press, 1992). In an earlier work, his authoritative study of Tan Kah Kee examines the pulls of loyalty and responsibility fully; *Tan Kah-Kee: The making of an overseas legend* (Singapore: Oxford University Press, 1987). But nothing captures the dramatic turn to the Chinese nation as well as 陈嘉庚 (Tan Kah Kee)'s own writings, notably his 《南侨回忆录》 [Memoirs of a southern huaqiao] (新加坡: 陈嘉庚, 1946). See also my essay, "南侨求学记: 不同的时代, 走不同的路", in 李元瑾 编, 《跨越疆界与文化调适》 [Crossing borders and cultural adaptations] (南洋理工大学中华语言文化中心 (Centre for Chinese Language and Culture, Nanyang Technological University; 八方文化创作室, 2008), pp. 13–28.

7. Tan Cheng Lock, *Malayan problems: From a Chinese point of view* (Singapore: Tannsco, 1947); Yeo Siew Siang, *Tan Cheng Lock: The Straits legislator and Chinese leader* (Petaling Jaya: Pelanduk Publications, 1990); Oong Hak Ching @ Ong Hap Ching, "Pengkajian beberapa aspek masyarakat China Peranakan di negeri-negeri Selat, 1900–1940", M.A. thesis, Faculty of Art and Social Sciences, Universiti Malaya, 1981.

8. There have been several studies about this since the early research by Yeo Kim Wah, *Political development in Singapore, 1945–55* (Singapore: Singapore University Press, 1973). For example, Michael D. Barr and Carl A. Trocki, eds, *Paths not taken: Political pluralism in post-war Singapore* (Singapore: NUS Press, 2008); Tan Jing Quee, Tan Kok Chiang and Hong Lysa, eds, *The May 13 Generation: The Chinese middle schools student movement and Singapore politics in the 1950s* (Petaling Jaya: Strategic Information and Research Development Centre, 2011); and Kah Seng Loh, Edgar Liao, Cheng Tjiu Lim and Guo-quan Seng, eds, *The University Socialist Club and the contest for Malaya: Tangled strands of modernity* (Amsterdam: Amsterdam University Press, 2012).

9. The complexities of the time are explained in Hong Lysa and Huang Jianli, *The Scripting of a National History: Singapore and its pasts* (Hong

Kong: Hong Kong University Press, 2008). The controversies arising from the Nanyang University tragedy has not died down as can be seen in the online site <https://www.sginsight.com/xjp/>. A recent study focused on the university's relations with the Singapore government, 周兆呈 (Zhou Zhaocheng) 《语言、政治与国家化: 南洋大学与新加坡政府关系, 1953–1968》 [Language, politics and becoming national: Nanyang University's relations with the government] (新加坡: 南洋理工大学中华语言文化中心、八方文化创作室, 2012). But the issues that aroused great passion at the time have now been redirected more towards a China that has joined the global economic system and is working with the United Nations Organization framework. This is a China that tries to project new kinds of modernity that respect enduring non-Western values. Identifying with this China will call on fresh thinking on the part of all those who say that they are Chinese.

10. This is a topic that has gained a following in recent decades and is centred on the new interest in Sinophone studies, Shu-mei Shih, Chien-hsin Tsai and Brian Bernards, eds, *Sinophone studies: A critical reader* (New York: Columbia University Press, 2013). Of particular interest for Singapore and Malaysia, E.K. Tan (Eng Kiong), *Rethinking Chineseness: Translational Sinophone Identities in the Nanyang Literary World* (Amherst, NY: Cambria Press, 2013).

11. Singapore leaders have explained this position eloquently in many writings, not least those by Lee Kuan Yew. Other alternative views of the Chinese position in such a pluralist environment may also be found. With emphasis on the past, Tan Jing Quee and Jomo K.S., eds, *Comet in our sky: Lim Chin Siong in History* (Petaling Jaya: INSAN, 2001); Said Zahari, *Dark Clouds at Dawn: A political memoir* (Kuala Lumpur: INSAN, 2001). With the future in mind, Ho Kwon Ping, *The ocean in a drop: Singapore, the next fifty years* (Singapore: World Scientific Publishing, 2016).

Chapter 7

HERITAGE WITH HISTORY

The Chinese neighbours that I grew up with in Ipoh, Malaya in the 1930s and 1940s practised different sets of family rituals and practices. Through these acts, they felt connected with the past as immigrants from China. Done regularly, that provided many occasions for the community to come together. Living in Singapore for the past twenty years, I note how some similar activities perform the same role today. In addition, I am happy to see that the National Heritage Board and various community organizations are doing more to alert people to the value of their cultural artefacts. That, however, is not enough if there are no parallel efforts to connect key aspects of Chinese heritage with knowledge of the historical conditions that produced them.[1]

Like other communities, most Chinese see their heritage as relevant to their lives but are not always aware that it also represents the living past. It is relevant because it is closely related to their migratory traditions within the region over the

---

This is a revised version of the keynote lecture, "Heritage and History" that I gave at the 3rd Heritage Science Conference on the theme, "The Treasure of Human Experiences". It was held at the Nanyang Technological University, Singapore on 25 January 2016.

past two centuries as well as to the homes in China from where their ancestors had come. Conscious or not, what they practise and what they respect, including what they are learning from past experience, is part of their heritage. It would be a pity if the heritage's links with history are taken for granted. A better understanding of the linkages should make their heritage more meaningful to their lives.

For some fifty years, experts at UNESCO have helped the world to think of heritage sites and practices as part of the heritage of humankind. These experts have a strong sense of history, and we are thankful that they have thus enriched our lives. In particular, they have demonstrated that protecting one's heritage can improve our appreciation of what is now being lost and forgotten. Their work reminds us that familiarity with history is essential if we are to appreciate what heritage means.

We all hope that modernity and globalization have softened the differences among the peoples in Asia, but it is obvious that, where heritage is concerned, distinctive attitudes remain. Singapore is no exception. The multiple cultures of its peoples are separate from, if not at odds with, one another. The island's brief past since independence has led people to identify with values that make them modern and global. That has meant setting high educational goals aimed at ensuring material success. That is understandable, but the city-state had for decades paid inadequate attention to the study of history and is only beginning to appreciate its importance. The neglect has made it harder for younger generations to realize that all talk about heritage is superficial and abstract if it is not connected with the people and events that produced it.

HERITAGE IN MODERN SINGAPORE

Singapore is a city with a high level of cultural complexity. For heritage here to be seen as important, there needs to be a keen awareness of the past experiences that impact on the present and still make a difference to people's lives. They involve the relationship between people and their pasts, including practices and artefacts that are intangible. In the context of Chinese attitudes towards heritage, let me take an example that illustrates the deep gulf between the ways different peoples can engage their past. In the Greco-Roman tradition that evolved in Europe, it was important for the Parthenon in Athens to be authentic, even if the original is in ruins.[2] In contrast, for the Chinese, the buildings on temple sites were often destroyed and rebuilt and were not valuable in themselves.[3] It does not matter that the original is no longer there and the current structure is only a copy. What counts is the relationship of people to the site. As long as the site is thought to be sacred, the building on it is the valued heritage. Such a perspective may be intangible. What is important for most Chinese is that the site's assumed sacredness could produce a tangible heritage. That way, they have inherited a cultural complex that is the product of centuries of mixtures and integrations, one that has never stopped adapting to changing circumstances and new challenges. The Chinese recognize that there are varieties of historical artefacts, some to care for and even profit from and others that are simply put aside. It is a dynamic evaluation of heritage that sometimes appears inconsistent and liable to misinterpretation. That, however, should not deter us from trying to explain it.

In Southeast Asia, most Chinese are descendants of men who came from different towns and villages in Fujian and Guangdong provinces during the past two centuries. Until the end of the nineteenth century, the men left home in pursuit of trade or in search for work. Their homes were far away from centres of power in northern China and they had a sense of belonging to small communities with distinctive cultural values, their local *xiangtu wenhua* 乡土文化. These bonds of beliefs, rituals and practices that were brought to the Nanyang were not totally sacrosanct. They could, if necessary, be modified to serve the needs of their multifarious enterprises and protect their lives abroad. Whenever the sojourners chose to settle down, they gathered together with kinsmen from the same district who spoke the same dialect. They built temples or shrines that gave them an added sense of security and identity.[4] When their groups became larger, they organized other bodies to represent their needs and expand their common interests. They were surprisingly innovative in adapting to local conditions, and this enabled many of them to prosper over the centuries.

Let me illustrate this adaptability with the example of the use of surnames. The Chinese were the first people to use the surnames of male heads of households to bolster the power of elites families. The oldest genealogy is that of Confucius' Kong family, now in its seventy-seventh generation, with a total of some two million descendants.[5] Out of over 5,000 surnames in use among Chinese today, it is estimated that the most common twenty of them add up to about 60 per cent of the population.[6] Over the centuries, following strong lineage traditions, these surnames steadily spread from the elites to other social groups, including non-Han peoples who immigrated to Chinese lands. By using a common surname as the basis for forming associations, each group that shared a surname was enabled to claim shared ancestors and thus strengthen lineage cohesion. These associations today can cross boundaries, local, national and global, and can when necessary enable strangers to make new contacts.

Confucian scholar-officials were particularly keen to recognize this kind of linkage as the central platform for social and institutional continuity. With this kind of inclusive relationships, people from localities far apart were thereby connected. Same-surname genealogies thus identified all who had the same surname as descendants of real or imaginary ancestors. That way, cooperative networks were readily established. That practice became widespread among ordinary people at least since the Song dynasty a thousand years ago. Every Chinese soon learnt to be creative to establish new relationships that could extend their community networks.[7]

The Chinese also have other forms of associations, most commonly those based on having the same district origins and sharing the same speech groups. Of particular importance is when they also worshipped the same local gods. From the very beginning, the sojourners and settlers learnt to employ these bodies to help their multiple operations. When abroad, these organizations were flexible enough to have overlapping memberships and many Chinese sought membership in more than one group. Where surname associations are concerned, it is remarkable that, while the retention of one's surname is tangible, the idea of surname bonding, whether the kinship was genuine or fictitious, is not. It is possible, when mutually agreed, to modify the terms of kinship even where there is no evidence of blood ties or any credible descent lines. When expedient, it is possible for surname identification to be relaxed in order to strengthen the range of social and economic activities. And, where necessary for smaller surname groups to stand up to more powerful ones, it was possible for people with different surnames to come together in order to further their interests.

The surname organization is portable, and travels easily with most Chinese. It can overcome barriers of sub-ethnic identity based on district and dialect differences and enable new networks to be created. Remarkably, surname bonding does not need to be locally grounded or externally validated because it even works when Chinese far away from their homeland wish to connect with same surname associations in China. Today, in a modern and global world, this heritage is no longer essential and certainly not as effective as in the past. But it is interesting to see how it remains an ingenious way of using the idea of common surnames to extend the basis for practical relationships.

This is but one example of intangible heritage being adapted for use outside China to support the kinship level of operations, serving as a kind of premodern non-governmental organization (NGO). There are other kinds of organizations that have the capacity to function widely outside their original environment and can be used to build networks to reach out to different countries and continents. What is more, this heritage is also useful for Chinese in China who want to extend their operations overseas and those who deal with foreign Chinese seeking to do business in China.[8]

At a higher level of responsibility, there is the example of what Chinese people have been taught to expect in the sphere of moral and competent administration. This heritage derives from the idea of a golden age when the ruler–subject relationship was based on having wise, caring and just rulers. That ideal became central to what Confucius taught when he set out to help rulers to govern well. Over the centuries, with increasing literacy among the people, the ideal percolated down to become part of people's dream of good rulership, even when local officials were avaricious and emperors were far away. However remote the hope, that ideal was part of a common heritage. What is surprising is to find it present among people whose distant ancestors settled outside China.[9]

The early male migrants to this region married local women and their descendants settled in various parts of the region. Their families in Singapore, often identified as Peranakan or

Straits Chinese, are similar to other communities in Malaysia and Indonesia, lands that were once under Anglo-Dutch commercial and colonial influence. They developed their own brand of heritage that combined Chinese artefacts with those of the Malay world. What gives that heritage its distinctive quality is the mixture of customary practices pertaining to birth, marriages and death, and their ingenuity in adapting to local food and dress. In addition, the community also has a clear grasp of the importance of social and family relationships drawn from their Chinese ancestors. The hybridity of that heritage is unique, and it has now been duly recognized in the Singapore story. Observers have been struck by the resilience of the Chinese elements in the heritage despite the fact that these Chinese have been cut off from China and spoke Malay and either English or Dutch and very little Chinese, if at all.

The way the males settled and learnt to identify with local elite life is an extraordinary story. In the Straits Settlements under British rule, they were proud to demonstrate their intertwined cultural preferences and even their allegiance to British imperial splendour. No doubt many had good reasons to be grateful for the opportunity to prosper outside China but their adaptations remind us that most Chinese abroad during the Qing dynasty (1644–1911) felt no commitment to Manchu authority that they considered alien and illegitimate. Instead, they depended on their own resources, including what they believed was admirable in their ancestral culture. Over time, however, there emerged among them a newfound respect for the effective way the British governed their colonies. In particular, they were won over by the British idea of an open trading world in which colonial laws could, when skilfully interpreted, give them a chance to develop their businesses. I do not mean that they admired colonial rule itself, or its capitalist ideology, or the racism and cultural superiority that came with it. Their respect was for predictable and orderly governance, and it was enhanced by their appreciation of an environment in which the merchant was not looked down upon as they were in China.

The response of these Chinese demonstrates a willingness to identify with a heritage of good governance. It came from their profitable experiences with British officialdom but, interestingly, it also drew from values that were found in the ideal of the "Confucian merchant" that they were taught to admire. This was a model built on ideals of filial piety and loyalty to the ruler, and acknowledged the five principles of benevolence, righteousness, ritual correctness, wisdom and trust. For merchants, they recognized that trust (*cheng* 诚) was a very important, if not the most important, value in their business dealings. This model became prominent in China during the sixteenth century. It gained acceptance when educated people no longer shunned those merchants who accepted the supremacy of classical Confucian doctrines. It was a development that merchants in China applauded and successful merchants made every effort to conform to its demands. Significantly, those who settled in the Nanyang were familiar with that model. They adapted it to apply to their relations with local rulers wherever appropriate, as in Vietnam, Siam and Java, and certainly did so in their relations with Dutch and British colonial authorities. This was invaluable when the model helped them to demonstrate their familiarity with Chinese elite culture. It helped them gain a degree of respect from the European counterparts with whom they did business.

In Singapore, the adjustments made by various Chinese communities to satisfy the governance methods of the Straits Settlements were constantly evolving to meet the rapid changes occurring since the mid-nineteenth century. As large numbers of newcomers arrived from China, as advances were made in global maritime transportation, and as China underwent political and social revolution, these Straits Chinese had to find new ways to deal with the challenges.[10] The elite groups that emerged in the twentieth century were further tested by the Japanese invasion and occupation. The defeat of the British and the Dutch brought new uncertainties to their world. After the end of World War II, in the face of rapid decolonization and the rise of conflicting nationalisms, everyone of Chinese descent in the region knew that they were in for a torrid time.

By the 1950s, a new generation of leaders have had to learn from a wide range of political challenges never experienced before. They had to deal with new kinds of contests for power and influence among different peoples, including among other Chinese with different ideological orientations. This was especially obvious in Singapore. Here the Chinese majority population faced a post-colonial plural society with unusual expectations. They had to determine what had to be done when the British left and local leaders had to shape a city into a nation-state.

It is remarkable how the new elites of independent Singapore combined key features of British colonial rule with selected elements of Confucian values for that purpose. They focused on what had to be done to ensure the economic future of a tiny state with no natural resources except an excellent harbour. They had to offer a law and order framework that was not backed by imperial power. They had to sensitize the people to a unique mix of interfaith and multicultural relationships. And, most of all, they had to provide the state with skilled manpower. Where this was concerned, they used the model of a mandarinate selected through examinations that was rooted in Chinese tradition. Singapore proceeded to educate its people to acquire the skills the country most needed. And, not least, it adopted modern professional training designed for a post-colonial plural society.

The application here of two distinct heritages is an example of tangible innovation, but the idea that past experiences with different origins can be mixed and adapted to drive present actions is no less imaginative.

Taken together with the multiple networking strategies brought by early Chinese immigrants that have taken root here, this governance-centred heritage has been reinforced during the past fifty years in Singapore's new developmental state.[11] Both are examples of using past experiences to cultivate new relationships. They show how Chinese outside China have been creative whenever they sought to be upwardly mobile and become modern and global. What is also interesting is that there are signs that the mixed heritage that brought new immigrants and local-born communities together have now become appealing to young people in China who have learnt to look outward. The new generations who experienced the disruptions and discontinuities under Maoist China are impressed by how the past can be actively present no matter where Chinese people have gone. They are beginning to see that the experiences of Chinese who have settled for centuries abroad can be relevant to their ambitions in China to achieve their own distinctive modernity.

HISTORY IN CHINA

The Singapore Chinese examples lead me to compare what history means in China where their heritage originated. This goes beyond the changes to the traditional kinship system following the revolutions that deliberately created new kinds of social and institutional relationships. It also goes beyond the national structures and modern administrative models that had aroused great expectations. At the heart of the link between heritage and history is China's ancient literacy. The efforts to connect its store of documents and records over three millennia played a critical role in shaping what became China and in determining who are Chinese.

Heritage in China has a long history although the idea that Chinese history is continuous has often been challenged. It is remarkable how official historiography has systematically ensured that China is defined by an unbroken continuity. For example, Chinese leaders are aware that modern Eurocentric world history has greatly impacted on the Chinese sense of their past. This began at the turn of the twentieth century when the country's elites discovered nationalism and internationalist communism. That was followed by the war against Japan in 1937–45 that turned nationalism into the new foundation for legitimacy for any Chinese regime. Chinese leaders now realize that it is one thing to inherit the mantle of an ancient civilization and another to build a progressive republican nation-state. They are still debating how to move towards an inclusive multicultural nation and avoid becoming an exclusive ethnic nation. The striking feature of most of the discussions is that they have never failed to use the heritage of unbroken historical continuity to help them decide what they should do.[12]

At its base is the heritage of records systematically selected and preserved for over 2,000 years. What holds them together is the intangible idea of *shi* 史, a word that we translate as history. But the word *shi* or *shi*-history referred to something more than history as times past or the writings that historians produce. *Shi*-history was the name given to the large body of knowledge that began with the *Book of Documents* (*Shangshu*), and the *Spring and Autumn Annals* (*Chunqiu*) that Confucius had compiled from the records of his state of Lu. This kind of *shi*-history included all varieties of documents and commentaries concerning every aspect of governance. Every dynasty after the unification of the

Qin-Han empires had dedicated officials appointed to collect and organize these records. Together, until the twentieth century, these records gave shape and substance to what we call China. They formed the body of knowledge that represented the collective memory of what China's rulers and mandarins did, and enabled future generations to ensure that the Chinese civilization-state continued to appear unitary and advance in the same direction.

This idea of *shi*-history has many facets. One of them, how heritage and history interact, is particularly relevant here. It demonstrates why history is important to people who identify as Chinese. Over the centuries, Chinese elites have tried to transmit everything that they considered significant by distinguishing and ordering different kinds of knowledge. After centuries of debate, they agreed to classify everything under four major categories, in the following order: first, the Classics encapsulating the key principles for Chinese elites to follow; second, the *shi*-history as the totality of the practice of governance; third, residual areas of practical knowledge, including philosophy and religious texts; and last, other forms of literature and individual collections of writings.

Throughout two millennia, the least controversial was the category of *shi*-history that brought together the whole story of China's dynastic rule. *Shi*-history was a mirror of government behind which was a deep respect for ancient ideals and models where ancestors were given a sacred place. In a similar way, everyone was exhorted to connect with ancestors to ensure empathy with cosmic order. Central to this order were the lineages and surnames within the extended clan-families, the successive dynastic histories in the imperial realm, and the notion of tributary relationships in the world beyond. Together, they gave rise to the ethical and political concepts that many still find relevant to China today.

The importance of *shi*-history was widely acknowledged as early as the Han dynasty. But there was no agreement as to which body of ethical and spiritual texts should serve as the source of all wisdom, something comparable to the Vedas in India or the Torah, Bible and Koran as the Holy Book. After several centuries of debate, during which claims were also made for Buddhist sutras and primary Daoist texts, the Chinese eventually settled for a set of new interpretations of the Confucian Classics. That was in the Song dynasty during the eleventh and twelfth centuries. The annotated Classics agreed upon then became orthodoxy during the Ming dynasty in the fourteenth century. And in the eighteenth century, the *siku* 四库 (Library) of the four categories of knowledge produced the Imperial Catalogue, the so-called Emperor's Four Treasuries. By that time, these Classics were identified as the bearers of China's core values. And next in importance was *shi*-history. Significantly, both were portrayed as beginning with Confucius, the Classics following his teachings, and the *shi*-history originating from the Spring and Autumn Chronicles that he had compiled.[13]

When the dynastic system was ended in 1912, the Imperial Catalogue was put aside. After two revolutions, in 1911 and 1949, two generations of Chinese leaders set out to replace the Classics with something modern and credible. There were efforts to do it with Sun Yat-sen's *Three Principles of the People,* and later, with Maoist communist teachings based on Marxist-Leninist doctrines. Neither was successful and it would appear that the task of establishing a new set of Classics is still continuing in China today. But there has been no disagreement that history (now *lishi* 历史) remains central to China's identity. Different groups of modern historians are still arguing whether to adopt Marxist or nationalist historiography to rewrite the past, but they all agree that history remains at the heart of the distinctive Chinese civilization-state.

In short, history in both its traditional *shi* and modern *lishi* form is an overarching heritage. The very idea of China depends on continuity with the ancient past. People are Chinese because they are descended from mythical lines of ancestors and they have therefore given a sacred place to ancestors. The first legendary rulers provided models of good rulership, and later lineages highlighted how such rulers had ensured the vitality of society as a whole. Some modern historians have questioned the authenticity of the records that perpetuate such beliefs, and scholars in every field have mocked the blind faith and superstition behind popular renditions of gods and sages. But the nationalist turn of the twentieth century led Chinese leaders to ask what ideals could best strengthen cohesiveness among their people. In the end, they have resorted to new interpretations of their heritage that are not dissimilar to what their imperial and mandarin predecessors had done. They have reselected from what they take to be the country's collective memory in order to establish new narratives. This now includes new archaeological finds and access to foreign archival materials, but the skeletal frame remains the one that was shaped by the past records of *shi*-history.

Obviously, Chinese people are expected to live with a keen sense of the past. This does not mean that they have to be acquainted with the actual records and the volumes of historical interpretations. Very few people would read them. What is in their consciousness, however, is the idea that the past is related to their identity and linking up with that past is necessary if they want to trace the source of what makes then Chinese. That heritage may be intangible, but it has constantly been replenished and revivified and unlikely to go away.

Many Chinese today are aware that the heavy burden of the tangible past of monuments and artefacts can be too much of a good thing. Others feel that the past should not be allowed to stand in the way of economic development, and whatever is necessary to provide modern standards of living to everyone. The rival appeal of the idea of progress is too great. Thus, there is a concern to balance a useful past with the urgent need to become a prosperous country. This has led to many contradictory moves. For example, historic buildings have been torn down to widen highways and replaced with multi-storey offices and residences. Sometimes, reproductions of traditional houses are built on the town's edge to cater to the tourist trade. Some cities and towns have preferred authenticity and kept the old centres. They chose to conserve the tangible heritage by building new towns a few miles away and move their offices and shopping malls to the new centres.[14]

It is interesting to see how the Chinese sense of the past operates at several levels. For most people, respect for the past is accompanied by calculations of what parts of it are worth keeping, while looking for practical ways to make heritage useful. At another level, faith and spiritual needs determine how they should respect the sanctity of select sites and plan their new urban surroundings to reflect that. Among officials, heritage can also be helpful if it reminds them of the ideals and standards of governance that people have longed for. At the highest level, caring for heritage could ensure that what is preserved would conform to the sense of continuity that legitimates the modern state today. At all levels, when there is too much past, Chinese people are pragmatic. They agree that heritage has to be selective and will be preserved only if it is meaningful and, better still, usable. Nevertheless, there is keen awareness that a sense of history is essential if the heritage that they respect is not hijacked and abused.

The Chinese experiences with their past show that there is no clear line between what is genuinely memorable and what has direct impact on policymaking and public behaviour. Heritage that is rooted in cultural values does influence those in authority. It can also have economic value and help improve people's well-being. But, for most people, when they see how heritage can help them relate to who they are and the way they live, they would see a place for such heritage in their lives. And this is likely to continue whether they are modern Chinese in China or a more complex mix like those among many Chinese in Singapore and elsewhere.

I began by saying how the efforts of UNESCO and similar bodies have helped to make people attentive to cultural heritage. That work is indeed important. But we need to be reminded that there is more to heritage than looking out for things that fit a list of cultural criteria. It is also necessary to examine how people relate differently to past experiences and to ideas about their past, whether tangible or not.

Singapore's Chinese are not any different. They know how to use an ancient artefact like a surname to support new dynamic relationships. Their ancestors carried their hopes for good governance out of China, and that inspired later generations also to seek it in a modern state. Today, they are sensitive to the rise of China and can see the role of history in shaping that civilization as well as a new national identity there.

In Singapore, heritage clearly matters. People are now more aware that past experiences can teach them what works and what does not. Heritage requires people to know and think about the relative value of different artefacts of their past, whether tangible or intangible. Their heritage shows them how their ancestors innovated whenever necessary in order to survive and prosper. But it is not enough to depend on personal instincts and group activities. We must know what enables us to recognize the parts of heritage that are meaningful. For that, it is essential to encourage the young to know their history, whether in their classrooms or in their surroundings.

I have taken Chinese examples to show their links with China where history is taught at every level and is deeply embedded in people's lives. But Singapore has its own distinctive history. It cannot afford to allow other histories to define heritage for its peoples. It is quite right to ask people to stress commonalities and not the differences. But there is no alternative to diversity here. And to respect diversity requires great sensitivity and that can only come if people know what the differences are and where they come from. New nations cannot afford to turn their backs on the past. It is only when they understand their heritage will they be able to imagine how they can shape a distinctive future for themselves.

Notes

1. The Singapore Heritage Society founded in 1986 has done a great deal to fill the gap, and the conference it organized in 1994 was an excellent wake-up call. That was before I came to Singapore. When the papers were eventually published in 1999 as *Our Place in Time: Exploring heritage and memory in Singapore*, edited by Kwok Kian-Woon, Kwa Chong Guan, Lily Kong and Brenda Yeoh, they helped me understand the context of the concerns with heritage that followed. The Ministry of Education has been increasingly attentive to devising history courses that would appeal to schoolchildren. With an ageing population, there is also growing interest in what the past means and how the young could be encouraged to connect more readily with the elderly. <http://www.singaporeheritage.org/?page_id=1363>.

2. A fine summary of this perspective of the past can be found in John Griffiths Pedley, *Greek art and archaeology,* 5th ed. (New Jersey: Prentice Hall, 2012).

3. Examples abound. Perhaps the best-known example is that of the Temple of Confucius in Qufu where the buildings have been rebuilt numerous times during the past two millennia. The recent restoration of many buildings destroyed by Red Guards during the Cultural Revolution reflect a similar traditional respect for the "sacred sites" although today there is the added inducement of profiting from tourism.

4. A recent collection tells this story vividly for Singapore, Kenneth Dean (with Hue Guan Thy), *Chinese epigraphy in Singapore 1819–1911* (Singapore: NUS Press, 2017). It builds on earlier collections like that by Chen Jinghe and Chen Yusong 陈荆和、陈育崧，新加坡华文碑铭集录 [Collection of Chinese stone inscriptions in Singapore] (Hong Kong: CUHK Press, 1970).

5. The 2009 edition of the Family Genealogy of Confucius 《孔子世家谱》 in 80 volumes, under the general editorship of Kong Deyong 孔德墉 (Beijing: Wenhua yishu chubanshe 文化艺术出版社, 2009).

6. <https://web.archive.org/web/20090105171001/http://www.nciic.com.cn/yewufanwei-rksu-mfcp2.htm> (accessed 29 March 2012).

7. A useful summary of stories about Chinese surnames may be found in Russell Jones, *Chinese Names: The traditions surrounding the use of Chinese surnames and personal names* (Petaling Jaya: Pelanduk Publications, 1997).

8. While such organizations are still being used in the region and elsewhere for practical reasons, there are signs that younger Chinese in Singapore are less keen to use them to link up with ancestral homes in China, Yow Cheun Hoe, "Weakening ties with the ancestral homeland in China: Case studies of contemporary Singapore and Malaysian Chinese", *Modern Asian Studies* 39, no. 3 (2005): 559–97.

9. It is fascinating to find echoes of such expectations in Song Ong Siang, *One Hundred Years' History of the Chinese in Singapore.* See the annotated edition published online by the National Library Board in Singapore, 2016.

10. Wang Gungwu, "The Peranakan Phenomenon: Pre-national, Marginal, and Transnational", in *Peranakan Chinese in a Globalizing Southeast Asia,* edited by Leo Suryadinata (Singapore: Chinese Heritage Centre and National University of Singapore Museum Baba House, 2010), pp. 14–26. Included as Chapter 5 in this volume.

11. The fiftieth anniversary of Singapore's independence has led to the publication of a large body of writings that captures this government-centred heritage, see the 30 volumes of Singapore Chronicles published so far, including one on heritage by Kennie Ting, Director of the Asian Civilisations Museum (Singapore: Institute of Policy Studies and Straits Times Press, 2016–).

12. Brian Moloughney and Peter Zarrow, eds, *Transforming history: The making of a modern academic discipline in twentieth-century China* (Hong Kong: Chinese University Press, 2011); and the probing enquiries of Ge Zhaoguang 葛兆光 in 《宅兹中国—重建有关"中国"的历史论述》 [Home in China] (台北: 联经出版事业, 2011).

13. In 2016, I presented a paper in June on "Dimensions of Chinese Heritage" at the Royal Swedish Academy of Letters, History and Antiquities Conference on "What is China?" and, in September, gave a lecture on 《中国"史"的传统和意义》 ["Shi" history in China: tradition and meaning] at Qinghua University Institute of Humanities and Social Sciences Lecture. From the two, I have completed a paper on "Dispensable classics, indispensable history", to be published in another volume of essays planned for 2018.

14. Notable examples are the municipalities of Xinhui 新会 to the west of Guangzhou and Haining 海宁 to the north of Hangzhou. The plans for a new urban centre north of the old city of Chongqing and the announcement of the Xiong'an megacity south of Beijing suggest that China plans to scale up future urban concentrations.

PART THREE

Reframing Contexts

Chapter 8

REFLECTIONS ON DIVISIVE MODERNITY

Heritage can unite communities, but it can also divide different communities and even the people within each community. With the advent of modernity, other layers of complexity are added. When the quest for modernity puts great pressure on individuals and communities, it can bring greater intensity to existing divisions and also create new sources of division. The lecture I gave in honour of Herb Feith, a scholar who closely examined early political divisions in an independent Indonesia, gave me the opportunity to talk about modernity. I saw modernity as a goal that the peoples of different origins in Malaysia and Singapore, and elsewhere in Southeast Asia, wanted for their respective countries. But some aspects of the modernity ideal have not brought them shared values. On the contrary, they seem to have divided the peoples further during the first decades of decolonization.

This is a revised version of the Second Herb Feith Lecture, "Divisive Modernity in Southeast Asia". The lecture was organized by the Herb Feith Foundation of Monash University and was given in Melbourne on 28 June 2004.

These were divisions that Herb Feith and I have talked about the few times when we met. We were concerned about the divisions for different reasons, but we shared a common interest in how they reflect the problems that developing countries faced when trying hard to become modern quickly. His particular concern was the travails of Indonesia while mine began with the troubled start to the new state of Malaysia. For both of us, our interests included political and cultural issues among the Chinese, not least those influenced by post-revolutionary China.

I gave the lecture with a heavy heart. It reminded me that John Legge and I were among the last persons to see Herb Feith on the Monash campus on 15 November 2001, hours before he was killed in a tragic accident. We had just had a thoughtful discussion about the fate of Chinese communities in certain parts of Indonesia after the fall of President Suharto. John Legge's presence when we talked was important. Herb Feith and I had not seen each other for more than a decade and it was John Legge who initiated our meeting and gave me a chance to hear his views about the latest developments in Indonesian democracy. I vividly recall that last discussion we had before we parted. We touched on the subject of new kinds of divisiveness in Southeast Asian society. We had shared views about how these were caused in part by the different expectations that people had about the pursuit of modernity.

Curiously, it was also something concerning a particular example of divisiveness that we talked about when we first met in 1965. At our earlier meeting, the topic that engaged us was divided views of history. I had gone from the University of Malaya in Kuala Lumpur to Canberra in late May 1965 on my first trip to Australia. I visited Melbourne early in July and had the opportunity to visit the newly established Monash University Centre for Southeast Asian Studies that John Legge and Herb

Feith had founded. I had been hearing news of divisions at home between leaders in Malaysia, those of the Barisan Nasional in the federal government and those of the People's Action Party in Singapore. All this was in addition to the even fiercer divisions between Malaysian and Indonesian leaders about the formation of the larger Malaysian federation, although the shooting war was not on the peninsula but mainly along the borders of Sarawak and Indonesian Kalimantan. A month later, on the day I was returning to Kuala Lumpur, 9 August, I heard news of Singapore's separation.

DIVIDED VISIONS

I recall meeting Herb Feith at other times when we also talked about what modernity meant for our region. We compared views about the process that the various new states in the region seemed to agree was essential to progress. We noted how different Southeast Asian leaders were choosing divergent political and economic policies to attain modernity. There was no one path and the choices stemmed from varied historical experiences as well as different perceptions of need. But there seemed to be general agreement that modernity was a unifying force for their respective countries. The leaders also believed that modernization could be achieved through understanding and mastering the ideas and institutions from successful European nation-states. They expected that a state built on modern principles would help form a united nation and also bring prosperity to their people. Few of them were concerned that such quests for modernity could also lead to new kinds of divisions among themselves in ways unknown in premodern societies. Since Herb Feith and I first talked about this, we have both seen how some of the new nations displayed these divisions during this past half-century.

Perhaps I should not have been as surprised as I was that the topic of the price of modernity came up again when we met for the last time.

When I made my first visit to Monash University in 1965, I had just been reading Herb Feith's classic *Decline of constitutional democracy in Indonesia.*[1] I learned a lot from that book. I was also impressed by the fact that the university's new Centre of Southeast Asian Studies was already seen as one that would one day match the famous Centre at Cornell University. There was a quiet conviction on the campus that Australia was in an excellent position to study the region closely and a major centre was what should be aimed for. It should go further and try to become a centre for the region as well.

Coming from Kuala Lumpur shortly after the new federation of Malaysia was established, I was very sensitive to the strains of nation building that the states in the region were experiencing. The Prime Minister of Malaya, Tunku Abdul Rahman, announced in 1961 that he agreed to reconstitute Malaya by adding the remaining British territories in northern Borneo as well as the colony of Singapore to form a larger federation. Immediately, President Sukarno of neighbouring Indonesia accused the Malaysia project of being a neo-colonial plot. He ordered the new state to be attacked. The slogan he used was, *Ganyang* or Crush Malaysia, one that he used with greater ferocity for years up to the time of my Monash visit.

Meeting someone who had studied Indonesian politics so closely was, therefore, fortuitous. I was keen to tell him how the new federation was not only being struggled against from outside by Sukarno's *Konfrontasi* campaign that could not stop it from being born. There were also bitter debates within the country, one so divisive that it had led to race riots in Singapore the year before and threatened tense ethnic relations in some parts of

Kuala Lumpur. I described some of the political arguments that continued bitterly and openly even after the federation had been established. When we spoke, I did not anticipate that, while I was in Australia, the battle *after* merger had become so serious that Singapore was to separate just a few weeks later.

At the core of the challenge to the Malay leaders of the new state by Sukarno on the one hand and by Lee Kuan Yew on the other were opposing views of history that all three sets of leaders firmly held. In particular, they could not agree on how a modern state should be structured and how the society should be developed. It was significant that all the confrontations were couched in the language of modernity, especially those pertaining to political ideology and economic goals. What is more, the strongest protagonists were modernizers who wanted their countries to become modern quickly in order to match the prosperous nation-states of the West.[2] Their disagreements drove them to great lengths with the readiness to put away anything that they thought stood in the way of rapid progress.

We talked about how to interpret Sukarno's motives. What Herb Feith had written about the limitations of constitutional democracy formed part of the explanation. He described the conditions that produced the guided democracy that allowed Sukarno to proclaim, without challenge within Indonesia, that Malaysia was nothing more than a creature of neo-colonialism. He portrayed Malaysia as something that Britain and the United States had created to retain their dominance in the Malay world. He declined to see that there were local elite interests involved who saw colonial borders at that stage as negotiable. For them, negotiations among the elites of the former British territories were legitimate. In Sukarno's eyes, the differences were ideologically determined and those elite interests were either feudal or capitalist. Therefore, he saw his opposition as founded on the long-term interests of ordinary people. He was the true modernizer fighting not only against the old forces of imperialism but in the forefront of the struggle to build a new modernity for the region.

The leaders in Malaysian were equally adamant. They saw the federation as a step forward towards a stronger and more viable modern state. They were determined to reach that goal even if it meant burying their pride and seeking help from British officials who had previously been sceptical about their ability to build a nation on their own.

That was not all. Another kind of divided modernity had also begun to unfold within the new country even while the Malaysian federation was being established. This was a division that was taking place among the very leaders who had fought hard for the federation to be created. It was between those at the centre who held the reins of power in Kuala Lumpur and those on the periphery led by some of the leaders in Singapore, Sarawak and Sabah. Of course, there were vested interests and strong personalities behind the confrontations and the divisions could not easily be explained. But underlying that battle was a divided vision of modernity.

On one side was a conventional notion of the nation-state as one based on the ideal of one language, one religion and shared history. On the other side was a less well-defined idea of a plural society that could be the basis of a multicommunal state. For this latter group, their ideal of the federation was one that was multicultural, with multiple languages, religions and other traditions that would be treated as equal and given considerable autonomy within the state. Even as Herb and I were speaking that day in July in 1965, the divisions within the federation were heading towards dangerous communal tensions. Attempts to compromise were thought not to have gone far enough. The new state had to be based ultimately on the nation-state in the mould of the Western European states or the country would face the kinds of civil war that destroyed the unity of Cyprus, Palestine and British India (to name the most obvious examples).[3]

Within weeks of our meeting, Tunku Abdul Rahman agreed to Singapore's departure from the Federation of Malaysia, but kept the Borneo states in. Neither of us anticipated that the opposing claims to modernity could lead to such a division. I had observed the divisiveness intensify immediately after the federation had come into being but had not fully grasped how complex a common desire to become modern could become.

Although at our subsequent meetings Herb Feith and I did not talk about those divisions again, we did note that the divisions ended up surprisingly well for the elites of Singapore and, in different ways, also very advantageously for those in Malaysia. It looked like a case of "divided we stand", with both sides finding benefits from division.[4] Those of us who supported the creation of the original federation thought that the country would have a better future if it stayed united. But we have to admit that continuous divisions in the name of two kinds of modernity could have produced tragic results. It would appear that, when visions of modernity are divided as much as that, contrary moves would have to be made. Imposing unity by force might have enabled the federation to survive but it could also have led to the federation's total destruction.

When we met in November 2001, we did not refer to these matters, but we could well have noted that yet another set of divided visions had been played out in Malaysian politics during the past decades. This time the division came from pressures for change inside the country. These had begun following the Iranian revolution in 1979, aggravated by the historic rivalry between Sunni and Shi'a sects within Islam in the Middle East. Although that rivalry was medieval in origin, the impact on the Muslims in Malaysia was not. It involved modernists in the governing UMNO party and those who were drawn by traditionalism and were open to influence by the Parti Islam Se-Malaysia (PAS) opposition. Both sides were engaged in a struggle to install their respective versions of modern Islam as the national religion.

The division, as expressed by the protagonists, stemmed from debates about modernity.[5] The government was committed to harness the established religion of the majority to a modernizing state. It contrasted its reformism with the opposition's backwardness. In turn, the opposition leaders claimed to stand for a true Islam that cared for the weak and the poor, one that was closer to a modern welfare state than the corrupt state-centred system favoured by the government. Such contestations arising from divided visions of modernity were not new. It was not a question of determining who was modern and who was not, or even who was more modern. What was significant was that Malay leaders on both sides of the debate were using modern arguments to achieve the modernity they desired and decide how that modernity should serve their supporters. Of particular concern was also how free the people were to choose between the different claims to modernity that divided their leaders.

These were not the only divisions. Among the Chinese communities, too, what modernity stands for continued to divide them. For example, how best to educate their young was the divide that caused most pain to each family. National education sought more standardization of the school curriculum, while the desire for cultural survival depended on the survival of modern Chinese schools. That issue had been part of their internal political battles from the start.[6] While the specifics have changed, the fundamental divide remains lodged in different interpretations of modernity for Chinese living outside China.

PARTICIPATION

Another divide arose from the modern phenomenon of youth activism. This was also a subject that came up in my talks with Herb Feith. His pioneering work as Australia's first volunteer abroad in Indonesia, and the Australian Volunteers International that he initiated, alerted me to the kind of volunteer youth work that was attracting attention in Indonesia. That remains a testament of his influence outside the academic world. He made me aware that he was no mere academic who was content only to deal with the world of ideas and knowledge. He was active in another world where, away from his students and his classes, he devoted a great deal of his time and immense energy to work for a network of civil society groups on issues of poverty and injustice both in Indonesia and Australia. He was an inspiring figure committed to doing what he could for young people who sought meaning in a rapidly changing world by active participation. For that, he was not only admired by his peers but also by all who came in contact with him, someone who was deeply involved with the human condition.

The many groups of people in Australia and Indonesia who know his work well have recorded their appreciation in various memorial meetings after his death and have made many statements about the range and depth of his feelings for people. John Legge described him as a great teacher, almost in a religious sense, that he was inspirational. Another old mutual friend, Jamie Mackie, who knew that part of Herb Feith well and had shared some of his commitment when they were young, shared some of his experiences with me. He filled in the bits of Herb Feith's life before I knew him, adding another dimension to my understanding of him as a young activist. Jamie Mackie was concerned that young Australians may not be as inspired to do what Herb Feith did half a century earlier. He stressed Herb Feith's creativity, his readiness to find new ways to propel his students to improve their environment. This gave me perspective to the conversation that we had on his last day. Two of the words used to describe him stuck in my mind. They were the words "creative" and "religious".

Let me take the first word "creative" and follow it up the dialogue Herb Feith had with Professor Bill Liddle of Ohio State University a few days before he died. Bill Liddle has generously shared it by letting the journal, *Inside Indonesia*, publish it. The text below comes from part of a broader discussion about President George W. Bush's policy against terrorism. I shall not talk about American foreign policy, so the quote is not in context, but it illustrates a feature of modernity that is relevant here. Herb Feith said to Bill Liddle,

> My preoccupation, for which I found quite a bit of sympathy
> in Indonesia — I got back from there on Friday after four weeks
> teaching at Gadjah Mada [University] and a week in Jakarta — is
> with fashioning *mendayung antara dua karang* [steering between
> two rocks] strategies.[7]

In the context of the theme of divisive modernity, this wish to fashion a set of strategies drawn from the Indonesian saying, "steering between two rocks", strikes me as particularly fascinating.

I have suggested earlier that the divisions leading to the break-up of Malaysia in 1965 should dispose of any thought that modernity needs to be inspired by the success of European nation-state models. The nation-state that grew out of political conditions in Europe was distinct from the multicultural port cities and agrarian polities of earlier periods of history. In its modern form, an alternative to a nation-state may be found in the city-state that flourishes in Singapore. As a smaller version of the more complex multinational state, it can also be very strong. Thus the nation-state and a globally ambitious city-state can be two very hard places, and there is no comfort in being caught between the two. It is therefore interesting how the young in both countries are responding to the activism that is transforming societies elsewhere, not least in the immediate neighbourhood. That emerging activism, like for Herb Feith's students in Indonesia, may be compared with one of the strategies of *mendayung antara dua karang*, steering between two rocks, that comes from the Indonesian saying.

In recent decades, numerous young people in Southeast Asia have been drawn to work for non-government organizations (NGOs). These NGOs are providing new generations of men and women with opportunities to adapt to a world of civic awareness. In Indonesia, this has given large numbers of people the opportunity to obtain a measure of inner autonomy within a repressive state structure like that of President Suharto during his last years. This is not to say that the nation-state is being seriously challenged. But the Indonesian example suggests that, with greater participation of the young, the region may not be content with the narrow and exclusive nation-state model it started with after decolonization. Instead, the activist groups are showing how determined they are to master the democratizing forces that they are innovating for their purposes. They seem clear that they need to connect with their revived country directly and creatively, and navigate between powerful central elites and local centrifugal forces.[8]

This strikes me as the kind of division that will challenge our region for a long time to come. Seeing Herb Feith's dedication to the young workers for numerous NGOs in Indonesia took me to the work of colleagues who work on comparable problems with NGOs in China.[9] On one side is the ideal of an integrated monolithic state that combines its power with a self-conscious unifying tradition, in short, a stronger version of the modern nation-state. On the other is the interdependent world that is being networked together by knowledge and technology and bolstered by transnational and regional institutions. It is the informal globalization that seeks to make creative demands on national governments. In response, the nation-states on their part will each become more defensive and try to fight back.

This will make it likely that, from both sides, the world will become more critical of the young activism that has built up so many NGO's in Indonesia and elsewhere in the region. These activists will be pressured to take sides and they will have to be innovative and try harder to maintain their autonomy. The search for strategies to steer between two hard rocks seems necessary when the various NGOs encounter divided modernities, for example, the divisions that are found in alternative Islamic and Christian interpretations of modernity. Equally dangerous is the global struggle that has been given the name of "the war on terrorism". This struggle has been depicted as one between the forces of light and those of darkness, or between modernity and medievalism or the Dark Ages. The young Indonesians may not see it that way. For most, it is more a division between those in the West who believe that theirs is the light and those in various parts of Asia, and not least in Indonesia, who are still struggling among themselves to determine where the light is or even where to look. They would see that both sides are the products of self-righteous modernizing forces that sought to define the twentieth century. Thus the two hard places are being shaped by whatever power was available to the contenders. The divisions can be represented on one side by the overwhelming resources of the United States and its allies and, on the other, by the claims of an alternative modernity that depends on the asymmetric use of inexhaustible human sacrifices. Both are the products of the modernizing forces that, over the decades, have created new kinds of divisiveness.

THE SECULAR DIVIDE

This brings me to the other word "religious". It came up again in my last conversation with Herb Feith. After talking about his students in Jogjakarta, he quite unexpectedly asked me what I thought of the Falungong in China. His interest surprised me. For one thing, I do not remember ever talking about events in China all the times when we talked. The topic of Falungong as a religion interested him because of his deep concern for freedom and rights, in particular, the freedom to believe and practise one's faith. I did not know enough about the Falungong to pursue the discussion. But his question intrigued me and drove me to think about another aspect of the divisiveness in the modernity that many of us want for our societies. I refer to that between secularism and the world of religion.[19] This is now a serious problem in Indonesia where the official Pancasila doctrine, understood by many to be essentially secular, is being challenged as a theory that is inconsistent with people's religious faiths.

From my own study of Chinese history, it would appear that most Chinese people are this worldly without being consciously secular. They have an approach towards spiritual faith somewhat different from that of people brought up in the major organized religions of the Middle East, especially Christianity and Islam. The Chinese view places far greater emphasis on this world than the next. Indeed, they have over millennia arranged their religious ideas and practices in such a way that these have been primarily directed to serve the people in this world. Rightly or wrongly, for most of them, the idea of religion is not seen as an intense experience that commits someone to absolute truths or passionate causes, least of all to efforts to determine the best way to get to the next world. Their worldly attitude towards the next life can be comfortably placed in the context of modernization, but it does not help them to understand the idea of secularism. Here I refer to the secularism that emerged as one of the central concepts of the Western European modern experience.

European Renaissance and Reformation history has provided a definition of secularization that emphasizes the bitter struggle between Church and State. It is centred on the need for the modern state to be free from Church interference. I realize that there are many versions of this idea of separation and that some countries are more overtly ideological about this issue than others. Nevertheless, the idea of secularism has been depicted as one of the critical preconditions of modernity in the West. It is seen as having played an important role in shaping the modernity that the rest of the world seems to want. In history, this process was more the story of how to stop the bloody divisions between religions and eventually also those between State and Church. Although many would agree that Church–State separation has done immense good to social peace in the West, others have pointed to new divisions in some countries between the secular and the religious.

This background from European history is hard to fit into the relationship between religion and worldly authority in Asia, and this is especially true for China. Thus when I was asked about the Falungong as a religious faith, I was hard put to explain it in the larger context that Herb Feith had in mind. There has never been a separation of Church and State in China, largely because the Chinese did not have what the West calls the Church. It is possible to suggest that what is worldly in China is similar to what is the secular in the West, but it is hard to draw comparisons. For most Chinese, the Falungong is a new body of faith that developed out of certain social needs and drew on modern science as well as traditional spiritual and physical practices that its followers believe can help them restore their sense of morality and hope.[11] It first manifested itself as modern translations of particular *qigong* breathing exercises that groups of people would practise together. That seems to satisfy the needs of people who are living under great stress and wish to prepare themselves to face new tests of endurance, including ill health and ageing.

As the numbers of practitioners grew, controversies have arisen about some of the claims of Falungong leaders about their transcendental powers and how their teachings might prepare their followers for another world. In the eyes of some, this is taking the movement into the religious realm. At this point came what was seen as a show of social or even political power outside the Chinese leaders' central offices in Beijing. What followed has become very controversial within China. The central leadership ordered a national crackdown on the organization. The political leaders were not unanimous about the decision and it was certainly not a popular one. But once the crackdown began, it created fresh divisions within Chinese society that highlight the question of China's secularism as well as national policies towards all religions.

The freedom to choose one's religion today is one of the great freedoms that modernity seems to offer. A country's policy towards religion is widely seen as a marker of the kind of secularism that empathizes with people's spiritual needs. However, China's socialist ideals have always been couched in terms of an absolute scientism. The first generation of revolutionaries and those who captured power in 1949 espoused the view that only science could save China from the kinds of superstitions that had led to the country's failure to modernize on its own.[12] They believed that a scientific ideology was the answer and the current leaders still see their responsibility as one to end all superstitious beliefs and practices so that the country can become vital and progressive. This looks like a kind of fundamentalist worldliness. It certainly makes it difficult for the Communist Party to deal with anything that is deeply spiritual, particularly ideas about salvation and the next world.

This is not the place to deal with Chinese religious attitudes, but the subject can be linked with the strategies needed to steer between two hard places discussed earlier. The Chinese government sees the Falungong as representing the dark forces of the past in its insistence that its strong faith could resist the lights of a communist future. But, by claiming to be scientific, Falungong can also be seen as a challenge to scientific socialism and another source of division within modernity. This is a reminder of how easily the earnest quest for the modern can turn into divisive and dangerous forces. Here I shall simply stress the divisiveness of absolute secularism that is different from the secularism that emerged in Europe. There in the West, to secularize helped to bring toleration and harmony between religions and this still has great appeal to its modernist admirers. Theirs is a secularism that stresses freedom and the respect for the rights of those who believe in different faiths. But that is the version that may characterize a softer modernity. The harder version however, uses the quest for scientific truth to reject anything that cannot be proven through reason, logic and experiment. It is this latter that could produce an extremism that does not tolerate religious faith at all and threatens the spiritual life that most people need. This can harden into a position that could deny the country the social harmony that the Chinese are proud to proclaim as their goal. Thus, it could also discredit the secular modernity today's China claims to uphold.

CONCLUSION

Whether modernity is divisive or not is a question that reminds us how philosophers have been debating issues of the absolute and indivisible for a long while. People like Isaiah Berlin tell us that there are some values that everyone should acknowledge as absolute. I am persuaded that it is legitimate to proclaim that certain values like human rights, freedom, equality, love of peace, and the need to believe in one's own faith (to take a few examples) could be seen as absolute. This does not mean that they constitute the core of every definition of modernity. Even if they were key parts of how modernity is represented, that would not make modernity absolute and indivisible. On the contrary, values that are absolute would have always been true and would therefore strictly speaking have nothing to do with becoming modern. At most, we can say that modernity has made it easier for some of these values to be realized and sustained in our globalized world. But it can also be demonstrated that the achievements of modern science and technology could also make us less free and equal, and even less peaceable.

Most Asians have always lived with both the worldly and the otherworldly and can go on living comfortably with them both. They have been fortunate that, with a plethora of religions that are available, there has never been a powerful Church that they would have to struggle to secularize. It seems to me a mistake to think of religions in Asia in that secularization framework and allow any idea of absolute modernity to emerge. Herb Feith's question about religion in China is a good reminder that modernity is a dynamic phenomenon and will always be work in progress. I think he would sympathize with any effort to steer between the hard rocks of all dogmatic claims for modernity. He would have agreed that it would be foolish to allow any absolute notions to dictate to modern lives today.

Notes

1. Herbert Feith, *The decline of constitutional democracy in Indonesia* (Ithaca: Cornell University Press, 1962). It was a time when most people agreed that every country should be democratic but were divided as to how elections should be conducted and who should get to vote. We were also just discovering how unprepared most people were for the divisiveness of election campaigns.

2. The following two sets of political thinking remind us what key leaders in Indonesia thought about the modern nation-building, probably the most challenging part of the modernization process, Herbert Feith and Lance Castles, eds, *Indonesian political thinking, 1945–1965* (Ithaca: Cornell University Press,1970); Leo Suryadinata, ed., *Political thinking of the Indonesian Chinese, 1900–1977: A sourcebook* (Singapore: Singapore University Press, 1979).

   For Singapore, the heat of battle is captured in Lee Kuan Yew, *The battle for a Malaysian Malaysia* (Singapore: Ministry of Culture, 1965). For Malaysia, we have the mature reflections of the former Prime Minister, Tunku Abdul Rahman Putra al-Haj, *Looking back, Monday musings and memories: The historic years of Malaya and Malaysia* (Petaling Jaya: MPH Group and Star Publications, 2011).

3. Further thoughts on what was misunderstood at the time about the history of nation-states are found in my essay, "What if the nation-state is no longer the key organizational unit of the international community?", *Singapore Perspectives, 2017: What If?*, edited by Gillian Koh and Debbie Soon (Singapore: Institute of Policy Studies and World Scientific Publishing Co., 2018), pp. 19–30.

4. See Chapter 2, "The Call for Malaysia", in this volume.
5. Farish A. Noor. *The Malaysian Islamic Party PAS 1951–2013: Islamism in a mottled nation* (Amsterdam: Amsterdam University Press, 2014); Joseph Liow Chinyong, *Piety and politics: Islamism in contemporary Malaysia* (Oxford: Oxford University Press, 2009); Julian C.H. Lee, *Islamization and activism in Malaysia* (Singapore: Institute of Southeast Asian Studies, 2010).
6. Lee Ting Hui, *Chinese schools in Peninsular Malaysia: The struggle for survival* (Singapore: Institute of Southeast Asian Studies, 2011); 叶翰杰著, 《挑战与回应 : 21世纪华小展望研讨会资料汇编》 [Challenge and response: Conference Materials concerning Chinese primary schools in the 21st century] (吉隆坡 [Kuala Lumpur]: 马来西亚华校教师会总会, 2001); 《与时俱进, 永续发展》 [Moving forward with the times, continuous development] (加影 [Kajang]: 马来西亚华校董事联合会总会, 2008).
7. Bill Liddle and Herb Feith exchanged views a few days before Herb's death, early in November 2001. They discussed the 9/11 attack on New York's Twin Towers, "Bush, Osama and the planet", *Inside Indonesia*, Edition 70, April–June 2002.
8. There are now about 1,000 NGOs in Southeast Asia. I was drawn to this subject by Mansour Fakih, *NGOs in Indonesia: Issues in hegemony and social change*, Occasional Paper Series on NGOs, University of Massachusetts Center for International Education, 1991.
9. Zheng Yongnian and Joseph Fewsmith, eds, *China's opening society: The non-state sector and governance* (New York: Routledge, 2008); 刘培峰, 谢海定主编 (Liu Peifeng, Xie Haiding), 《民间组织发展与管理制度创新》 [Development of NGOs and new systems of management] (北京市: 社会科学文献出版社, 2012).
10. Mayfair Mei-hui Yang, ed., *Chinese religiosities: Afflictions of modernity and state formation* (Berkeley: University of California Press, 2008); Herbert Fingarette, *Confucius: The secular as sacred* (New York: Harper & Row, 1972); Wang Gungwu, "Secular China" (Giri Deshingkar Memorial Lecture), *China Report* 39, no. 3 (July–September 2003), reprinted in Gregor Benton and Liu Hong, eds, *Diasporic*

Chinese ventures: The Life and Work of Wang Gungwu (London: RoutledgeCurzon, 2004).

11. Benjamin Penny, *The religion of Falun Gong* (Chicago: University of Chicago Press, 2012).

12. Julia Ching, *Chinese religions* (London: Macmillan, 1993); Paul R. Katz, *Religion in China and its modern fate* (Waltham: Brandeis University Press, 2014).

Chapter 9

END OF EMPIRE

Dividing empires into new nations was a major political gift of modernity in Southeast Asia. These empires have been a very large part of my life ever since I became aware of the world around me. My parents talked about the Dutch, the British and the Japanese empires incessantly when I was a boy. Both of them were born in Qing China, an empire on its last legs. They were conscious that the end of that empire simply meant that China was at the mercy of other empires. They had grown up with the threat of the Japanese empire spreading from Korea to Manchuria, and poised in North China ready to invade the rest of China. But there was nowhere else for them to turn to get away from empires. After graduation from Southeastern University in Nanjing (itself once an imperial capital), my father was offered a job to go to the Nanyang to educate the children of overseas Chinese. He went to work, first in British Malaya and then in Dutch Java, both

This is a slightly revised version of the keynote lecture given on 1 February 2006 at the conference on "Southeast Asia: Past, present and future" in honour of Nicholas Tarling's seventy-fifth birthday held at the University of Auckland. It was subsequently published as "Southeast Asia: Imperial themes", *New Zealand Journal of Asian Studies* (June 2009), pp. 36–48.

places ruled by Europeans who were confident that their empires would go on indefinitely. But even there, there was already the growing shadow of a powerful Japanese empire.

Thus, when I first met Nicholas Tarling over fifty years ago, I was struck by how he was immersed in the study of empires in the Malay world in which I had grown up. I had found the British and imperial history I was taught at school difficult to like. At the time I met Nick Tarling, I was looking forward to the decolonization taking place that would bring that history to an end. Therefore, I was intrigued to meet someone who was so deeply interested in the imperial story. Nick Tarling went on to devote his professional life to describing those empires. He was not content to study British power at its peak but followed the story to the retreat of all Western empires after the Japanese defeats of 1942–45. He then went further to examine the various ways each of the empires was wound down and how some of them developed other power systems to deal with the region.

Ever since I met Nick Tarling, I was conscious that his life and mine were entwined with empires in strangely different ways. Thus when I was invited to give the keynote lecture at a celebratory conference addressed to him, I thought I could be somewhat more personal than normal. It is with that in mind that I linked the theme, "Southeast Asia: Past, Present and Future", to the person whose seventy-fifth birthday was being celebrated. I doubt I can satisfy anybody with what I recall but will try to pursue some of Nick's and my own experiences with imperial themes in Southeast Asian history. I shall not only talk about the past. I also hope to show that there are imperial themes in different contexts and different kinds of empires.

Many of us wish to see the end of empires forever, and indeed some kinds of empires may have come to an end. But imperial themes are pervasive and resilient and may be more present than we think, and more relevant for the future than we would want. I recall suggesting a few months ago, when commemorating the end of World War II in Asia, that the kind of empire that the Japanese had tried to establish in Southeast Asia between 1941 and 1945 was gone and never to return.[1] My audience thought that was wishful thinking and pointed out other imperial possibilities that might be subtler but no less imperial. I agree, though I still think that the old-style territorial empire that the Japanese tried to create will not be repeated. Indeed, the word empire is used today for many things: not only political entities but also business, financial, media and cultural empires and there are vague but cognate concepts in words like neo-colonialism and neo-imperialism. I do not, however, wish to get into those areas here, but will concentrate on empires that project political power and influence.

Nick Tarling is a son of the British Empire while my father was born just before the collapse of the Manchu Qing Empire, both once powerful albeit in quite contrasting ways. However, I grew up in Malaya as a subject of Britain's global outreach, so there are some differences and similarities in Nick's and my perspectives. Thus, in approaching the topic of imperial themes, I shall begin with some reflections drawn from our two life experiences of empire from the centre and from the edges. After that, I shall explore three sets of changes and talk about

(1) empires becoming colonies,
(2) empires becoming nations, and finally,
(3) nations becoming empires.

I shall then end with some reflections on future imperial themes.

Let me begin with the two of us finding ourselves in Southeast Asia. Nick started as a historian when the modern British Empire was still actively transforming itself into a commonwealth of nations. Britain was in the midst of orchestrating the establishment of a new class of sovereign states that would be friendly to their former imperial master. Nick would have studied in school the formative years of that empire, and probably a fair amount about the classical Athenian, Persian and Roman empires. Along the way, he was likely to have compared British imperial progress with those of Britain's rivals. I do not know how much a classical scholar he was in school. If he were one, the rhetoric of the Roman Empire at its height would have shaped the language and imagination of the budding historian.

Also, I know how much Nick loves the theatre. If that love had come early, then I would expect him to have absorbed the imperial cadences in Shakespeare's powerful words (and the images they conjured), from plays that I had also read, like *Henry V*, *Julius Caesar*, and *Anthony and Cleopatra*. When I think of Nick having done all that before he first stepped into the British archives, I can see why he is such a dedicated historian. I even wondered, had he been born earlier, whether he would have been content to be a historian of empire, whether he would not have been an empire-builder himself. Why act on a stage when you might have been, if not Stamford Raffles or James Brooke or Frank Swettenham, at least George Orwell or Leonard Woolf?[2] Nick, in any case, came on the swelling scene in time. He studied with Victor Purcell at Cambridge, and Purcell would have provided him with a rich personal perspective of the British Empire in multi-communal Malaya/Malaysia,[3] when the last generation of imperial officials staged one final dramatic effort at state building in Southeast Asia.

In comparison, my imperial experiences were somewhat miscellaneous. I was born in the Netherlands empire in the East Indies and grew up in Perak when it was a British quasi-sovereign protectorate. As a schoolboy, I always wondered what was being protected, British imperial interests or a nominal Malay sovereignty. Our school observed Empire Day and the King's/Queen's birthday. But we also did obeisance with calls of Daulat Tuanku (Long live the King!) when Sultan Iskandar Shah (1918–38) or his successor Sultan Abdul Aziz Shah (1938–48) or their representative in our Kinta district, the Raja Bendahara, visited the school. From 1941 to 1945, there was an interlude during which I encountered the Japanese empire. Perhaps it was not typical of all empires at war, but I learnt from those three and a half years how bad empires could really be if they tried, and also how short-lived some empires could be. When that ended in 1945, the British returned — not quite in a blaze of glory, but they showed us how adaptable and resilient they were by setting out to reinvent what they were preparing to leave behind.[4] I was never sure that we were being "decolonized", it felt more like we were "deimperialized". So I had a second dose, this time of a chastened imperial power divesting itself of the burden if not the memory of empire.

My early education was a mixed bag, and the imperial themes of my youth were confusing, even contradictory. The only constant was that I learnt and lived through enough to question the glories of empire and welcome the end of empires. For example, the only history I remember learning in secondary school was that of the British Empire, taught out of a very dull textbook[5] by a teacher who was dutiful but obviously bored. The only correctives for me came from two sources. One was the Chinese classics that my father taught me during the Japanese occupation that introduced me to some notions of an ancient empire in China.[6] The other was from the stories I heard from my Malay friends in school about the Malacca Empire from which the state of Perak claimed to have been descended.[7] Thus I was not in any way prepared for the serious study of history and the thought of being a historian never occurred to me.

When I first met Nick, he was in the enviable position of having direct access to the rich archives that all historians dream of. He had just started publishing then but, as we all know, he has over the past fifty years made excellent use of these archives in the most systematic way. This was a great time for the imperial historians of Western Europe. There was a closure. The story, after centuries of splendid as well as dubious beginnings, now had an ending. The five acts were all there, the bodies could now be counted and the historian was ready to step up to say his piece as the curtain came down. In this case, he was free to analyse pithily the great and foul deeds or to draw a moral lesson for our times.

My fate was different. My generation in British Malaya was being prepared to face a new beginning, a nation-state modelled on those in Europe but, unlike them, given universal suffrage from the start, with our multiple communities filled with great hopes and even greater anxieties. Malaya was to be an example of what Rupert Emerson called the process "from empire to nation".[8] But before I confronted that process, I had gone to China to study in the National Central University at the capital of a dying regime, the Nationalist government of Chiang Kai-shek. I was witness to a recently failed empire that was also a failed state still struggling to build a nation.[9] In order to avoid being caught in the civil war that the Chinese Communist Party was to win, I returned to Malaya. The new Federation was then in the midst of a communist insurgency that challenged the kind of state that the British wanted to set up. At its climax, this had led to the killing of the British High Commissioner, Sir Henry Gurney, in 1951. Despite that, I was introduced to a hopeful experiment, to British ingenuity busily nation-building on the foundations of a colonial state.

At the University of Malaya in Singapore from 1949 to 1954, I was fortunate to study with two remarkable historians. One was the historian of British India, Eric Stokes, who probed the underpinnings of the ideas behind Victorian imperialism. The other was Cyril Northcote Parkinson, the naval historian, who traced the decisive factors in British trading power that led them to Singapore and the opening of the China market.[10] However, my taste for British imperial history had been killed at school. So I chose a different tack. My stay in Nanjing had drawn me to a puzzling question, why did the Chinese empire not simply become a nation-state in the first half of the twentieth century? So I began to study that generation in China who helped to abolish the ancient empire and got it to rename itself a republic. Not only did this empire fail to become a united nation, but the nascent republic was also dogged by civil wars and foreign invasions. As a result, only a small part of its records were preserved and what survived in the archives between Taipei and Beijing was not open. In addition, with the communist victory in China in 1949 and the anti-communist war in Malaya, it became impossible for me to study modern China without being suspected of harbouring "terrorist" sympathies. By 1953, I was determined to be a student of history, so I chose to examine the nature of the ancient Chinese empire instead, with an eye on the relations of that empire with Southeast Asia. Thus Nick and I, coming from different directions and looking at different time-scales, came to meet in Southeast Asia/Nanhai/Nanyang.[11]

EMPIRES BECOMING COLONIES

Let me now turn to my first point about empires becoming colonies. Neither of us did research on the native empires of the region. We studied empires that had strong state foundations elsewhere whose origins and trajectories of growth were quite different. Nick's world was global with many nation-state protagonists each capable of reaching out faster and further than before. By the end of the eighteenth century, the British East India Company had consolidated its trading empire beginnings and was on the verge of transforming itself into a national empire built on industrial capital. As for me, I looked at a continental Chinese empire that consistently turned landwards. Even though it never lost its trading links with Southeast Asian ports, the Confucian state did not encourage state-to-state relations. It chose instead to slot Southeast Asian polities loosely into a tributary system that was originally invented for China's own internal use and thus kept the relationship somewhat feudal between rulers. All the same, both Nick and I were aware that there were native imperial themes at work in the region and followed the work of our colleagues with great interest, notably historians like Georges Coedes and Oliver Wolters on the Hindu-Buddhist states, scholars who did so much to stretch our imaginations about the imperial functions that these states performed.[12] It was not a coincidence that we both concentrated on maritime Southeast Asia. This was the easternmost part of the British Asia that Nick focused on. I, of course, was born and grew up in the middle of that Malay world.

You may have noticed that I have used the word empire for very different kinds of states and that I was careful not to use its twin, the word imperialism. In fact, the definitions of empire are many because there have been so many empires in history but many of them could not be said to have been imperialist. Historians and political scientists have argued endlessly about what is common to all of them. For example, what do the ancient empires of India, China and Persia have in common with the modern British, Dutch and Japanese empires of the nineteenth and twentieth centuries? I shall come to that later. What about

those empires in premodern Southeast Asia? The word empire
has been used readily in our history texts today for the Angkor
(or Zhenla-Khmer) and the Siamese empires on the mainland and
Sri Vijaya, Majapahit and Malacca empires in the archipelago.
One might add Vietnam moving south towards Cambodia if
only because it is a reminder how elastic the term empire can
be. There were empires to which other states paid tribute that
also offered tribute to the larger Chinese empire.

I must admit I knew little about the local imperial polities
before I went to university. I should have known more about
Malacca. It was the closest both in geography and in spirit to
the state of Perak where I went to school, but most non-Malays
of my generation knew less about that empire than about the
Portuguese capture of its capital in 1511. It took me years to
understand the significance of Malacca's links with the empire of
Sri Vijaya and its relations with the imperial states of Java, Siam
and Ming China, and even longer to realize that, as empires, all
these were very different from one another. I need hardly say that
the European and Japanese empires that I had personally lived
under were not at all like any of those mentioned.

As we know, parts of these empires ended up as examples of
European colonies. But what do words like empire and colony
mean here, especially when they are juxtaposed? If what the
Portuguese strung together in the sixteenth century across wide
expanses of ocean was an empire, and similarly what the Dutch
did the next century was another empire, what does it mean to
say that Malacca was a Portuguese colony and Batavia a Dutch
colony? In fact, the Malay and Javanese empires did not disappear.
The names changed and their centres moved but the traditions,
the claims, the aspirations, and even the core elites, could trace
their roots back to the same imperial origins. In a tradition that
emphasized a mobile core, one empire's centre could become

another empire's periphery and be regarded as the latter empire's domain. When threatened or defeated, new imperial centres could be found, established and defended afresh. Thus the empires of the archipelago had their own characteristics.[13] Oliver Wolters decided to give them a special name. Inspired by the stories of several Sri Vijayan capitals that were precursors of the later Malay capitals, both on the peninsula and widespread across the Java Sea, Wolters turned away from conventional references to vassal and satellite polities, and drew analogies with the concept of the mandala polities of South Asia. His analyses were most enlightening, but nothing could detract from the fact that the overarching frame he used was imperial, even if uniquely so.

This is not the place to debate the semantics of empire. For maritime Southeast Asia, what was striking was the imperial mobility made necessary by weak state structures. A system of portable institutions was feasible because they were built on maritime trade. Such institutions appeared soft and plastic but they were stuck onto lightly assembled and resilient frames. In that way, people, genealogy and economic performance were more important than location and longevity. The loss of a port-city was replaceable, and sacred sites could be reconsecrated elsewhere. Clearly this was not the norm when compared with the larger and more stable empires of the period, but its strategy of survival persisted through the early centuries of European expansion from the sixteenth to the eighteenth centuries.

The land-based empires on the mainland did not support this form of imperial agility. The Hindu-Buddhist Khmers, as also the Sailendras in Java, did move their centres from time to time, but their monuments were more grandiose and permanent and had to be fiercely defended. Similarly, the Vietnamese came south and took the lands of the Cham rulers, and employed the highly structured model of the Chinese. They too settled for imperial grandeur. As for the empires that succeeded the Khmers and the Mons on the Menam and Irrawady valleys, the Siamese and later the Burmese did no less to fortify each new city as they expanded their respective realms. They were thus less vulnerable to the modern maritime powers that came from the West who, in any case, had obtained enough of what they wanted from the Malay networks of the archipelago. The mainland empires were therefore not challenged for over 200 years. Only a new kind of empire would want to try to breach their walls. This was eventually developed in Europe by the British and the French during the nineteenth century, the product of high industrial capitalism. And it needed their brand of overwhelming power to turn these native empires, with the exception of Siam, into what was to be called colonies, in these cases, really subjugated states.

EMPIRES BECOMING NATIONS

This takes me to the second idea of empires becoming nations. I lived through the years of global decolonization and observed the process of turning former parts of empires into new nation-states. Nick's work on Britain's efforts to decolonize while seeking to retain residual influence as long as possible was exemplary in reinforcing the image of orderly imperial retreat. I was so impressed by British success compared to Dutch failures in Indonesia and the French disasters in Indochina that I took for granted that that was the ideal way for empires to disband. More than that, the British Empire withdrew to become the Commonwealth of Nations. Despite adopting the broader Commonwealth name, Britain's homeland remained but a nation-state. Thus empires not only spawned nation-states but could also return to being one again. I found this intriguing because it was clear that this did not apply to empires that had never been nation-states in the first place. I was thinking of the China that I was trying to study. Sun Yat-sen and his Nationalist Party thought they could take off their imperial coats and raise the republican colours, and thus make China a new nation-state. What they did not expect was that the national empires that impinged on China's sovereignty at the time saw China as a dying empire that could be reduced to several nation-states. By their definitions, there was "China Proper" and there were the others that all qualified to be nation-states by right. Of course, unlike the maritime empires, adjacent territories on the edges of empire were more difficult to detach. Britain looking north from India and Russia looking south from Siberia challenged each other to do just that and the stalemate between them helped to save territories like Tibet and Xinjiang from being removed from China. And between French and British competing interests, most of the original province of Yunnan stayed within Chinese borders. In that context, the Russians did help establish the Mongolian republic and the Japanese colonization of Taiwan has left a separation that haunts China still. On the other hand, the rival ambitions of the Russians and the Japanese prevented China from losing the provinces of Manchuria permanently.

As it happened, it had not been possible for me to do research on modern China in Malaysia. So I looked at the Chinese empire in its trade with the Southeast Asian ports of the South China Sea. They led me to the origins of the tributary system devised for a *tianxia,* or "All Under Heaven", that John King Fairbank called "the Chinese world order".[14] This new term suggests that, by the criteria that defined empires in European history, China was not quite the kind of empire they were familiar with. All the same, as shorthand, everyone used the word empire for China until 1911. What is interesting is that, long after 1911, the shadow of empire still seems to follow China around. No matter that, officially, all countries recognize China as a large multi-nation state and accept its international borders, it has been easy for regions like Southeast Asia to be pointed to as targets of a future "China threat" because of its imperial past.

It is true that the Qin-Han Empire advanced into the Red River valleys of northern Vietnam over 2,000 years ago and stayed over 1,000 years. It is true that, over a long period of some 600 years, the kingdom of Dali and the tribal statelets of Guizhou and Yunnan were gradually incorporated into what became Ming and Qing imperial provinces. It is also true that vague terms like feudal and tributary relations, vassalage and suzerainty, left us unclear whether they might be used again in future relationships. I had gone on to study North China during the late Tang and Song dynasties, covering a long period when the Chinese empire was weak and divided. This was when Chinese emperors were sometimes forced to pay tribute to other emperors stronger than themselves.

My study led me to examine other manifestations of empire in Asia. For example, the Mongol conquest of China under the Yuan dynasty led to aggressive activity in Southeast Asia, including the invasion of Burma, Vietnam, Champa and Java (and Korea and Japan as well). The climax of these actions came after the Mongols were driven out when the Ming emperor Yongle sent the eunuch admiral Zheng He on naval expeditions to the Indian Ocean and the coast of East Africa. I studied the reasons for Emperor Yongle's fleets to travel to and through Southeast Asia and it is clear that he had extended the tributary system across the oceans in an unprecedented way. The decision, however, was his and, after his death, there was no sustained interest in maritime affairs or in political relations. There remained some official trade with Southeast Asian kingdoms, but the only naval forces left were maintained to fight piracy on the Chinese coasts and, under the Manchu Qing rulers, to capture Taiwan from the Ming loyalists there.

This imperial theme touched the region lightly and surfaced from time to time, most notably when armed Chinese and Japanese trading consortia under Zheng Chenggong (perhaps better known as Koxinga) and his father had threatened the empire during the Ming-Qing transition of the seventeenth century.[15] After that, China passively accepted that several Southeast Asian ports were garrisoned by Europeans and was content to limit or deny these traders any rights in Chinese ports themselves. The lights of empire began to dim for China by the end of the eighteenth century although the mandarins were still unaware of the power shifts the British had made in the region. Yet it remained itself an empire where Manchu invaders ruled over the Han majority and the idea of nationhood as we understand it was not much more than a strong sense of multiple local Han ethnicities. Thus I came to understand how difficult it was for an empire to become a nation-state if it was never one in the first place. From that point of view, imperial Britain's experiments at nation building, however imperfect they have been, provided a far stronger base for nationhood than anything imperial China could have done for its own peoples. But, now that the Chinese are embarked on their nation-building tasks, will they understand what it means to be a mere nation-state? Will they be content to be that or will they learn from Europe and Japan that nations could be aggrandized to become empires?

NATIONS BECOMING EMPIRES

Let me now turn to how nations became empires and look at the changing imperial themes brought by the Europeans to Southeast

Asia. The earlier empires were primarily trading ventures initiated by kings or merchants before the age of nation-states. This was certainly true of the Dutch and English East India companies that competed aggressively in the archipelago. Each went on to take imperial shape and evolved imperial characteristics over a couple of centuries. Before the Dutch and the English, the Portuguese and Spanish did have missions that could be traced to deeper medieval roots. The Portuguese proclaimed to have come to the East in search of "Christians and gold", and this was also the understanding of the Spanish crown. This mission survived from the spirit of the Crusades, an outreach of the struggles over trade and the Holy Land. It gave the Spanish settlements in the Philippine islands a distinctive imperial theme that the Portuguese tried less successfully to match in their small toeholds off the coasts of India, China and the Malay Peninsula. The side commitment to find Christians, however, remained and served as an ideological sub-text common also to the European peopling of the Americas. It carried an imperial theme that was pre-national but was both universal and enduring, and elements of this mission to bring the truth to less fortunate natives have survived till the present day.

By the eighteenth century in Southeast Asia, the trading roles of the Dutch and the English had become dominant. Gold was acknowledged to have been more important than Christians, especially with the rise of the country traders bypassing the English East India Company. A century later, with the success of the industrial revolution in Britain, the shift was decisive and one could speak of capitalist empires in search of markets, primary resources and ultimately territorial control. This was certainly truer of Britain than of the Netherlands. The greater need to provide and support the factories of the former pushed the British to go further than any other trading empire in history. This is the story that Nick and his colleagues had to tell. Clearly, there were new imperial themes during the nineteenth century that transformed the nature of empire in Asia. The British led the way. They took on more onshore responsibilities in India and turned the tea and opium trade into *casus belli*, they dominated the maritime routes through Southeast Asia and subordinated the Chinese empire to a different imperial framework.

Economic power was the key, but the shift from commercial ventures to industrial needs, whether markets, mines or plantations, were not nearly as dramatic as what was the really new feature of the empires of the nineteenth century. Nick drew attention to this point in one of his earliest essays, written almost fifty years ago, "The relationship between British policies and the extent of Dutch power in the Malay peninsula, 1784–1871". I read this when I was still freshly under of the influence of C.N. Parkinson's majestic two volumes, *Trade in the Eastern Seas, 1793–1813* and *War in the Eastern Seas, 1793–1815*, about the rivalry between the two foundation nation-states of the modern world, post-Napoleonic France and Britain. Nick's thesis showed that the Dutch nation-state was thereafter adjunct to its larger neighbours and this determined the future of its empire in Southeast Asia. What really changed was that companies, merchants, wealth and profits were no longer the key determinants of power shifts. The consequences of British national victory over the French was the emergence of national empires, a model that spread the link between empires and national pride and glory to other rising nation-states in continental Europe and ultimately to the United States of America.

What are national empires? Aren't all empires national? Obviously there cannot be such phenomena before the creation of nation-states. For example, it would be totally anachronistic if not absurd to describe Sri Vijaya, Majapahit or Malacca as national empires. Similarly with the Angkor-Khmer, the Siamese or the Burmese. The only exception may be the Vietnamese because their identity hinged on differentiating themselves from the "Chinese". It did not matter to them whether Han, Mongol or Manchu elites ruled the larger empire to their north. Vietnam survived as what D.G.E. Hall called a proto-national state. Their later campaigns against the Cham states to its south eventually brought all Cham lands into the Dai Viet kingdom. Insofar as Vietnam was a proto-nation, that expansion might be comparable to the modern national empires that developed in Western Europe.[16] However, that did not save Vietnam from becoming part of the French empire in Asia, and France was unquestionably the classic national empire, something that Asia was only just beginning to encounter.

It is at this point that national imperialism was added to the original imperial themes. It not only had its source in industrial capitalism, as Hobson and Lenin were later to argue, but was strongly linked to the rising urge to national aggrandizement and ultimately to exaggerated claims to political, technological and even cultural and racial superiority. I emphasize the "rising urge" because I do not suggest that this was the origin of national empires. Commercial competition was central long before national pride and glory became factors in empire building.[17] It was only after the end of the eighteenth century that British national ardour to defeat and keep out the French, and then the German, the Russian and any other likely rivals, became a primary concern. And that was to engage Britain for the next 150 years. At first, Britain's Indian empire was the challenge, if not the only model, for other ambitious powers. But this developed into a British-led battle for greater share and control of the markets of China. Soon each European nation-state would join the race to capture as much as possible of that market before others arrived. In that context, Southeast Asia seemed to some to have become a sub-plot in the imperialist play.

However, Nick Tarling has written much on these developments to correct such a description. He unfailingly searched the archives to prove that the region was never a sub-plot but a key link connecting the new imperial themes of the nineteenth and the first half of the twentieth centuries. His series of studies took us step by step through all the ins and outs of the British Empire at its zenith, and they have provided much of the evidence we need to show that Southeast Asia was a vital part of the globalizing chain of modern empires. In so doing, he has also enabled us to read the writings of Eric Hobsbawn, Linda Colley and, more recently, Ben Anderson, with specific reference to the model of British nation-formation and the changing roles that new projections of imperial power played in the politics of the Malay peninsula and archipelago.[18] Nick has now followed that up with studies of later British efforts at state building in the Commonwealth and their belated efforts to decolonize the territories under their control or protection. The goal was to mould them into nations despite the harsh reality of having helped to draw new national borders with little historical validity.

Two of the imperial themes concerning nations becoming empires deserve attention. The rich documentation of national empire building is invaluable. How a maritime trading empire grew to become the world's greatest naval power had shaped the British imperial nation. That united and confident nation continued to grow almost unchallenged for at least half a century. It set high standards of national superiority, the idea that the nation-state was the most efficient instrument of imperial power. Some would argue that this also led to arrogance and complacency. Then came the challengers, all impressed by Britain's success and by the efficacy of the nation-state model. Several of these sought to become national empires themselves, notably industrial Germany, United States and Japan. Even the large and ponderous Russian empire expanded overland towards British spheres of control and influence only to be replaced by an even more threatening Soviet power. In short, national empires encouraged rivals who were intent on making their own nation-states stronger and greater.

The second theme could be framed as a question: will new aspiring nation-states have the capacity to be national empires in the post-Cold War world? The question has been asked since the European powers began to withdraw from their empires in Southeast Asia half a century ago. There was a rejuvenated nationalist China followed by a messianic communist China, there were international revolutionary movements within Southeast Asia that had attached themselves either to the Soviet Union or to the People's Republic of China. Although every nation-state rejected the idea of empire after the end of World War II, there are no guarantees that some imperial forms would not return or new imperial themes could not be invented. The most powerful nation-states after that war were the United States and the Russian core of the Soviet Union. Although in some eyes, one was benign and the other evil, how different were the two from behaving like national empires in the deadly rivalry that energized them?

What is at stake is the nature of the international system that was predicated on the general acceptance of nation-states as primary political units hereafter. When countries vary so much in size and power, it is difficult to believe that the system can ensure equality among nations. The example of a Western Europe weary of war and empire could be a catalyst to warn against future glorification of old nation-state values, but much more influential is the dynamic engine of growth provided by the United States that has already transformed East and Southeast Asia and seems willing to do the same elsewhere. With the coming rise of China and India, there is more economic growth forthcoming.

This brings me back to the contrasting experiences that Nick and I have been studying. On the one hand, there is the Anglo-American model sharing the outgoing European tradition of "Christians and gold" that had opened up the American continent and swept up on the shores of Southeast Asia. On the other, there is the populous Chinese example of a former empire yet uncertain about the kind of nation-state it expects to become. The former now has gold enough to turn attention to a mission of values. The latter still has to guard against making the same mistakes that new rising nations had made only a few decades ago. My study of Chinese history suggests that the lesson has been learnt, that China's acceptance of international norms comes not only from national interest but is also influenced by the system of political and social values that had shaped its relations with Southeast Asia for more than 2,000 years.

Southeast Asia's present is still based on how it adjusts to Asia's new confidence, how much to retain of its imperial experiences and how much it can organize its nation-states to deal with global markets and the national powers that could have imperial potential. It is unlikely now that its Asian neighbours will follow the nineteenth century European example of national aggression or the twentieth century revolutionary impulse to determine the regime changes of other nations. There has been enough history written about the horrendous disasters of the two centuries to alert the region's leaders to cooperate with one another. It is time to consolidate the regional groupings that could protect the region's long-term interests. The imperial themes that the region has been through have been varied. Their histories can be conjoined to help us outline some future scenarios. I believe Nick's birthday provided an opportunity to pool the many fields represented at the conference to reflect our present and help construct our future.

Notes

1. "Opening Remarks", in *Legacies of World War II in South and East Asia*, edited by David Koh (Singapore: Institute of Southeast Asian Studies, 2007), pp. 3–6.
2. The first two, Raffles in 1819 and Brooke in 1842, were empire-builders; Swettenham (1850–1946) was the epitome of the masterly colonial official who made sure that the empire was competently administered. As for Orwell and Woolf, both served the empire in Asia and wrote brilliantly about their imperial experiences.
3. Victor Purcell (1896–1965) was the most scholarly and prolific of the Chinese scholar-administrators of his generation. He was the expert on Chinese affairs in British Malaya and had written several books that gave credit to the Chinese contribution to the Malayan economy before he joined the teaching staff of Cambridge University. He was someone whom many Malayan Chinese leaders looked to for support when they felt that the majority of British officials were pro-Malay. I was one of many Chinese who learnt a great deal about ourselves through books like *The Chinese in Malaya* (Royal Institute of International Affairs and the Institute of Pacific Relations, Oxford University Press, 1948) and *The Chinese in Southeast Asia* (Oxford University Press, 1951). Although we did not necessarily agree with all his interpretations, we acknowledged his pioneering contributions. I was happy to contribute to the volume in his honour that Jerome Chen and Nicholas Tarling edited, *Social History of China and Southeast Asia* (Cambridge University Press, 1970), "China and Southeast Asia, 1402–1424", pp. 375–401.
4. I give examples of the departure arrangements that the British had made in Chapters 2 and 3 in this volume. I also suggest how some of these arrangements produced the power structures that have enabled the new post-colonial states of Malaysia and Singapore to succeed after independence.

5. James A. Williamson, *The British empire and Commonwealth: A history for senior forms*, first published in 1935. It was still the text for all schools in the empire and the Commonwealth in 1946, my last year in Anderson School. I later learnt that new editions were produced in 1948, 1954 and 1962 and again in 1964, the year the author died. For years, I would meet men and women schooled in Australasia, Africa and the Middle East who had learnt their history from Williamson's textbook.

6. My father was not interested in history itself but, in teaching me classical Chinese, he chose many texts, from the *Historical Records* of Sima Qian and the *Book of Han* of Ban Gu, that described the empire that emerged out of ancient notions of "All under Heaven" (*tianxia*), especially about the Qin and Han dynasties that established the dynastic system of empires that lasted for over 2,000 years.

7. We were not taught any Malay in school but my classmates told stories from the *Sejarah Melayu* (Malay Annals) about the heroic exploits of men like Hang Tuah who loyally served the Malacca Empire before its capital was captured by the Portuguese in 1511. This was meaningful to them because the rulers of Perak claimed descent from the Malacca royal house that escaped to Sumatra.

8. Rupert Emerson, *From Empire to Nation: The rise of self-assertion of Asian and African peoples* (Cambridge: Harvard University Press, 1960). Emerson knew Malaya well and had published a major study of British and Dutch colonial rule in the Malay world, *Malaysia: A study in direct and indirect rule* (New York: Macmillan, 1937). We had no chance to study politics or political science at the university, and read the book via my economics major where we studied economic development in Southeast Asia.

9. There are numerous studies of the second Chinese civil war of 1946–49. Among the recent studies of the period I lived through in Nanjing, two have been particularly enlightening, Long Yingtai 龙应台, 《大江大海一九四九》 (台北: 天下杂志, 2009); and Odd Arne Westad, *Decisive Encounters: The Chinese Civil War, 1946–1950* (Stanford: Stanford University Press, 2003).

10. Eric Stokes (1924–81) gave me a new perspective on British imperial history as he was working on what was to become his first book, *The English Utilitarians and India* (Oxford: Clarendon Press, 1959); while C.N. Parkinson (1909–93) was inspiring as a teacher of naval and maritime history, *Trade in the Eastern Seas* (Cambridge: Cambridge University Press, 1937) and the book he was finishing, *War in the Eastern Seas* (London: Allen & Unwin, 1954). I should also mention the lectures of Ian A. Macgregor that introduced me to the fascinating story of the early Portuguese and Dutch activities in the Indian Ocean before they built their empires.

11. My Nanhai trade study, ʻThe Nanhai Trade: A study of the early history of Chinese trade in the South China Sea", appeared in 1959 as a monograph issue of *Journal of Malayan Branch of the Royal Asiatic Society* (vol. 31, pt. 2, 1958), a few years before Nick Tarling's *Anglo-Dutch rivalry in the Malay world, 1780–1824* (Singapore: Donald Moore, and University of Queensland Press, 1962).

12. The many contributions of the two scholars have received the accolades they deserve. The two works to be singled out here for their remarkable insights are George Coedes, *Les etats hindouises d'Indochine et d'Indonesie* (Paris: E. De Boccard, 1948; earlier version published in Hanoi in 1944, further revised, 1964); translation as *The Indianized states of Southeast Asia* (Honolulu, East-West Center Press, 1968); and Oliver Wolters' seminal *History, culture and region in Southeast Asian perspectives* (Singapore: Institute of Southeast Asian Studies, 1982; revised edition, Cornell University Southeast Asia Program Publications, 1999).

13. The classic work of Anthony Reid pulls it all together, *Southeast Asia in the age of commerce, 1450–1680* (New Haven: Yale University Press, vol. 1, 1988 and vol. 2, 1993). There are important augmentations and afterthoughts in some of the chapters of *A history of Southeast Asia: Critical crossroads* (Chichester: Wiley Blackwell, 2015).

14. John King Fairbank's famous edited volume, *The Chinese world order: Traditional Chinese foreign relations* (Cambridge; Harvard University Press, 1968), popularized the idea of a "Chinese world order".

I contributed an essay to the volume but was unable to attend the conference at which the term was thoroughly discussed. Hence my hesitation to accept the term except as one that reflects the Chinese concern to have an orderly way of controlling their environment of a "Chinese world". My essay (pp. 34–62) dealt only with the background of early Ming relations with Southeast Asia, when the Ming founders were still struggling to restore Chinese pride after a century of Mongol rule over all of China, and trying to deal with what was at the time still the greatest land empire the world had ever known.

15. The latest set of papers to determine the significance of East Asian maritime power during the seventeenth century puts the story in perspective, Tonio Andrade and Xing Hang, eds, *Sea rovers, silver, and samurai: Maritime East Asia in global history* (Honolulu: University of Hawai'i Press, 2016). Another fine recent study is Cheng Weichung's *War, trade and piracy in the Chin seas (1622–1683)* (Leiden: Brill, 2013).

16. D.G.E. Hall was my official supervisor for my graduate studies at School of Oriental and African Studies in London (1954–57). The year after I arrived, he published the first edition of *A History of Southeast Asia* (London: Macmillan, 1955).

    I had written about Tang China's relations with its Annan protectorate in "The Nanhai trade" (1954, MA thesis for the University of Malaya in Singapore) and was very interested in how Vietnam became independent during the tenth century. He was the first person who made me think of Vietnam as a proto-nation, possibly the first "nation" in Asian history. Later, Keith Taylor showed convincingly that the Vietnam-China border is probably the oldest border that remained more or less unchanged for some 1,000 years, *The Birth of Vietnam* (Berkeley: University of California Press, 1983).

17. J.A. Hobson's convincing linking of capitalism with imperialism, *Imperialism: A study* (London: Nisbet, 1902), established a perspective on empires that influenced a whole generation of scholars. Vladimir Lenin turned that into a clarion call for revolution in his *Imperialism*

the highest stage of capitalism (1917). I do not deny that the connection between capitalism and imperialism was strong but this was separate from the emergence of national empires by the end of the eighteenth century.

18. Among the many scholars who have contributed to our understanding on the nation, these three are particularly relevant here. Eric Hobsbawn provided in his numerous writing a multi-angled perspective of all aspects of modern nation building in Europe, bringing them together in the 1985 Wiles Lectures, *Nations and nationalism since 1780: Programme, myth, reality* (Cambridge: Cambridge University Press, 1990). Linda Colley has given the most sensitive account of the complex factors that lie behind the formation of the British nation, *Britons: Forging the nation, 1707–1837* (New Haven: Yale University Press, 1992). As for Benedict Anderson, his contribution to how new nations, notably in Southeast Asia, find their way out of earlier political frames has been widely acknowledged as outstanding, *Imagined communities: Reflections on the origin and spread of nationalism* (London: Verso, 1983; revised, 1991).

Chapter 10

FAMILY AND FRIENDS
China South and Southeast

Countries in the Nanyang have always been conscious of China, more so when it is united and prosperous and less so when it is weak and divided. As more people study modern China's foreign relations, they have noted the rupture between its structure of tribute and trade or "the Chinese world order" and the new system of nation-states governed by international law. Chinese reluctance to accept the rules introduced by the Great Powers into Asia went through many stages, and it is only recently that the government in Beijing is seen to be functioning comfortably in the dominant United Nations state-system. It is possible to explain that change as inevitable. After all, in the world of nation-states, China has no choice but play by the rules that guide the actions of all other states. But the fact that it took China so long to demonstrate that it accepted the key aspects of the system and

This is a lightly revised version of the essay, "Family and Friends: China in Changing Asia", published in *Negotiating Asymmetry: China's Place in Asia*, edited by Anthony Reid and Zheng Yangwen (Singapore: NUS Press, 2009), pp. 214–31.

the fact that some neighbouring states in Asia still have doubts about China's future intentions suggest that the issues remain less clear-cut than might have been expected.

On one hand, the position that imperial China had insisted on in dealing with foreign rulers through the centuries was always accompanied by given sets of ritual, defined levels of hierarchy and agreed criteria of hegemonic authority. However, despite the sense of continuity that Confucian historians have given to the nature of Chinese dynastic rule, there was never any immutable structure of tributary relationships.[1] What seemed unchanging were the language of feudal condescension and the administrative rules drawn up by various Chinese courts to deal with power realities at different periods of history. Chinese rulers and mandarins had to be flexible in interpreting tribute relations according to the political, economic, security or cultural needs at any one time. They employed terms that appealed to forms of fealty, family or friendship with most of them interchangeable depending on circumstances.

On the other hand, the practical position China have taken since the second half of the nineteenth century was guided by principles of law incorporated into a modern system of nation-states introduced from the West. Despite the legal language that shaped modern international behaviour, the Chinese were painfully aware that much of that was subject to close examination and that, for each situation, there were always specific political, economic and security calculations to be made. There was always room for challenge and debate in concepts like equality, sovereignty, interest, pride, dignity, honour, morality, history, memory and leadership in inter-state relations.[2] In that context, successive Chinese governments during the twentieth century have accepted or rejected parts of the international law that the Great Powers have highlighted at different times.

Thus the Chinese have swung back and forth between moralistic and practical positions, and these swings reflect their struggles to emerge from a century of weakness towards the recent decades of growing strength. And, while a largely legalistic framework has replaced China's feudalistic approach, the reality for the modern Chinese state has never been neither moralistic nor purely pragmatic but the negotiable areas in between that directly influenced all power relations between nations. For the Chinese, navigating in those areas has been feasible and even reassuring because they have always found ways around the hard language of international law by continually using the more comfortable rhetoric of family and friendship.

During the second month of his Provisional Presidency in February 1912, Sun Yat-sen told an American reporter that his people could not understand why the Great Powers were not prepared to recognize his government in Nanjing. He was extravagant in insisting that there was no government in Beijing and in claiming that the Nanjing government ruled over 350 million people and its writ reached to the borders of Burma. He had made several personal appeals to the Japanese government. His foreign minister, Wang Chonghui, the first graduate of Beiyang College in Tianjin, was using personal connections to negotiate with his former teacher and president of Beiyang College, Dr C.D. Tenney, the American "special representative". But there was no response from Japan and no agreement was reached with the United States. All the foreign embassies waited in Beijing to watch future developments. They eventually recognized the Republic of China more than a year after Yuan Shikai took over as President. Sun complained, "The world was friendly, the Europeans were friends, we have friends everywhere, but we need recognition, you should recognize our government." Earlier, he had asked the French government "to establish friendly relations as two sister republics". But the law of nations was above family and friendship. None of the Great Powers made a move when they knew that Sun could not unite the country by force and that, in order to avoid a civil war that he could not be sure to win, he had to allow Yuan Shikai to take over the presidency from him.[3]

In the inauguration swearing-in speech he made early in January 1912, Sun had used more wishful traditional language. He spoke of combining the lands of the Han, Manchu, Mongol, Hui and Tibetan as one country and as one people. He described the five peoples as "one family" but urged all to work together so that the other states in the five continents would be more friendly and treat China as a fraternal state (*xiongdi zhi bang*) that was as close to them as lips and teeth. Elsewhere, he used more legalistic terms: in the new constitution of Sun's party, the Tongmeng Hui, promulgated in March 1912, its platform spoke of assimilating all the peoples of China into one nation and seeking equality among the nations of the world.[4]

Sun Yat-sen was the most modern Chinese political leader at the time and he had to struggle with a range of terms that mixed the familiar and the new in his addresses to his people. One can imagine how much more difficult it was for most other Chinese to envisage the position China was in with regards to the Great Powers and to its neighbours in Asia. But it was not a new problem. The problem had been there since at least the seventeenth century when officials who were tasked to write the history of the Ming dynasty (1368–1644) had included, in the section on foreign Asian countries, three European countries that had taken lands in Southeast Asia during the sixteenth and seventeenth centuries, like the Iberian states of Portugal and Spain (Folangji) and the Netherlands (Helan).[5] None of these could be said to have fitted into the tributary system that the Ming had designated as the basis for foreign relations.

In any case, Zhang Tingyu's final version of the *Ming History* was not published until 1739, almost a century after the fall of the dynasty. By that time, the Jesuits had worked at the Qing court and the English East Company had become a major player in Asia, and Manchu and Chinese mandarins were aware that the geography of China and Asia in the world was far more complex than they had once thought.[6] Although Qianlong Emperor's notorious words to Lord Macartney saying that China needed nothing from the West have been endlessly quoted to suggest that the dynasty was ignorant of what had changed in Asia, it would be wrong to think that the new developments had no impact on China's traditional tributary system. Although the framework and the official rhetoric were still in use, the key officials dealing with foreign relations had observed changing power relations in the maritime kingdoms and ports to China's east and south and were already aware of writings by travelers like Xie Qinggao, Wang Dahai and others.[7] Information gathered from foreigners meeting at the port of Guangzhou (Canton) in the early nineteenth century also enabled Lin Zexu, Wei Yuan, Xu Jiyu and others to prepare new studies concerning China's neighbours, like *Sizhou ji, Haiguo tuzhi* and *Yinghuan zhilue*. All these books incorporated new information about the rest of the world, but they did so with China's worldview still more or less intact.[8]

Nearly 200 years after the *Ming History* was completed, the loyalist former officials of the Qing dynasty published in 1927 the Draft History of the Qing dynasty (*Qingshi gao*) in which they outlined changes in the nature of international relations. A new section of eight chapters on the powers that had diplomatic relations with the Qing covered most of Europe and parts of the Americas but, where Asia was concerned, Japan was now listed with the other Great Powers. It had been loosely grouped with

China's tributary states in the past. Only four chapters at the end dealt with the rest of Asia. In three of them were the kingdoms of Korea, Vietnam, Burma, Siam and Laos. But, of the scores of tributary maritime kingdoms and ports that filled past official histories, only the island states of Ryukyu (Okinawa) and Sulu remained. The seven in Asia that remained were listed under the title of *shuguo* (tributary states or colonies), but it was noted that none of them were China's *shuguo* by the end of the nineteenth century. They had become the colonies of powerful countries like Japan, France, Britain and Spain. Only Siam was depicted as a former *shuguo* that had achieved self-rule or independence (*zizhu*) in 1852 through diplomatic negotiations between Britain and France. It is noteworthy that Korea was not recorded as a *shuguo* of Japan, another Asian state, but as having been amalgamated (*hebing*) with it. Why *hebing* was used was unexplained. These loyalist historians were compiling their work in Manchuria under the shadow of Japanese power and it is understandable why they had to be careful in the language they used when describing what the Japanese after the Meiji Restoration had done to Qing China, including annexing the province of Taiwan and *shuguo* like Ryukyu and Korea.[9]

Chinese leaders of the late nineteenth century found it difficult to believe that what had been an enduring set of feudal–personal relationships between their Son of Heaven and the neighbouring kingdoms and chiefdoms in Asia was coming to an end. The regulation of tribute and trade, after centuries of loosely defined multi-layered relationships, had evolved into an elaborate institution during the Ming and Qing dynasties (fourteenth to nineteenth centuries). The mandarins thought that this was a proven system that had gained respect for China and ensured China's security. Now that new forces were active in global politics and their system was no longer effective, Chinese leaders recognized that they had to follow the set of international laws that the Western powers applied to China. But their doubts about that framework remained for another century, especially when they found that these laws could not save China from continued threats of invasion and dismemberment and could even be used to thwart China's desperate efforts to reunify the country. What is more, they also learned that the laws were largely unenforceable when powerful states chose not to adhere to them. This confirmed that, in the end, China needed to regain wealth and power before it could count on the efficacy of law. In the meantime, to assist its survival as a unitary state, it would have to make use of informal appeals to friendship and familial ties among all states. Although these were not binding, they were more familiar to its Asian neighbours than the legal language of the West.

Immanuel Hsu, in his study of the years 1858–78, spoke of "China's entrance into the family of nations".[10] He did this in 1954 when the term "the family of nations" was taken to mean the group of nineteenth century Great Powers that had determined which countries were civilized enough to join their family and which were not yet ready. In the 1950s, China under the Chinese Communist Party (CCP) was freely using family and friendship terms in certain contexts. Among revolutionaries, words like comrade were common but, echoing older usage, there were also phrases like the brotherhood of man that knew no borders and, in particular, the relations between transnational communist parties that were described as fraternal. These words pertaining to family and friend could be interchangeable in Chinese. Close friends were likened to siblings though it was recognized that, between friends, there was a distance that needed additional mental and spiritual bonds if set against the demands of blood and kinship.

The family metaphor was popularly used in European international relations as well, especially before World War I when hopes for the peaceful resolution of Great Power conflicts were seriously disrupted. It remained among the other words that were used during the discussions leading to the Covenant of the League of Nations, including more formal and legally correct words like association, community, confederation, alliance, and society. The Chinese keenly followed this development. In their tradition, joining the family could be compared with joining the club in the English-speaking world, something China had not been asked to do. Both words conveyed warmth and intimacy and were appropriate in less formal celebratory occasions. But they also suggested tight-knit bonds that excluded those who did not belong.

When the CCP came to power in 1949, the People's Republic of China (PRC) was not able to join the family of the United Nations. Actually, Mao Zedong proclaiming at Tiananmen that the Chinese people had stood up was in a far superior position than Sun Yat-sen's thirty-seven years earlier. He had, like the great empire-founders in Chinese history, won total victory on the battlefield and held the Mandate of Heaven although the mopping-up job was not complete. The rival regime under Chiang Kai-shek after 1949 was far weaker than Yuan Shikai's in Beijing in 1912. But the Nationalist Government of the Republic of China was still a member of the family of United Nations, the new legitimizing body, and it was supported by the United States and had a Treaty of Friendship and Alliance with the Soviet Union. Hence Mao Zedong had good reason to feel insecure in the larger world family and wanted as soon as possible to sign a Friendship Treaty with the USSR and get Stalin to break off with Chiang Kai-shek. He thus adopted the idea of a socialist *family* of nations (*shehuizhuyi guojia dajiating*) by going to Moscow and signing the Sino-Soviet Treaty of Friendship, Alliance and Mutual Assistance of February 1950, an act that made the two countries "brothers in arms".[11]

This was a fateful decision. Within months, it led Mao Zedong to fight on the side of the North Koreans against UN forces led by the United States. This consolidated his identification with the communist or socialist family of nations headed by the Soviet Union. By limiting that family to nations that shared the same ideology and revealing the exclusive and defensive position of the PRC, it underlined the possibility of more than one family of nations. Of course, as demonstrated in the course of a decade, this was illusory. After the Sino-Soviet quarrel became serious in the early 1960s, the Chinese did not find the phrase "family of nations" comfortable to use for relations between nations. In addressing the developing nations of Asia, Africa and Latin America, they turned to other phrases like, "within the Four Seas, all men are brothers", or special relationships that are "as close as lips and teeth", and made general appeals to old and new friendships. When eventually the PRC was admitted into the UN and took its seat in the Security Council, it still hesitated to speak inclusively of the family of nations. And, for the first decade of Deng Xiaoping's reforms, friendship between nations was the preferred term.

Since the 1990s, the term family of nations has reappeared but is still sparingly used for relations among states. Only in the context of the UN family have the Chinese been uninhibited in using it. Nevertheless, its current informal use reminds us that, more than a century earlier, the Chinese had been forced to acknowledge that the structure that John K. Fairbank called "the Chinese World Order" had become obsolete. My essay in the volume focused on the institutionalizing of the mature tributary system soon after 1368.[12]

Almost exactly 500 years later, in 1864, Henry Wheaton's *Elements of International Law* was translated into Chinese. That translation showed how complex the new power reality in Asia had already become. It was a landmark not only for the Chinese but also for the Japanese who immediately reprinted it and adopted it for all their future diplomatic dealings, not least in advancing their interests on the mainland at the expense of China. The rules were those used by the family of Western Great Powers at China's gates. In the state-system where nations were seen as autonomous moral and political entities, the underlying principles were based on philosophical and theological traditions rooted in the Mediterranean and Atlantic worlds. Romano-Germanic legalism or Judaeo-Christian ideas of natural law had little in common with Chinese ideas that stress moralistic, voluntaristic, familial and hierarchical understanding of power, part-Confucian and part-Buddhist, that China and Japan shared to different degrees and in different proportions.

The Qing mandarins after 1864 struggled with the legal terminology used in *Elements* and tried to make the new words match those that they had invented for their ancient tribute-trade system. Some officials still thought that there could be more than one family in the world of nations. But after the Qing fell and dynastic China came to an end, the Republic of China from 1912 (on the mainland till 1949 and in Taiwan since then), as seen above in the pleas by Sun Yat-sen, sought desperately to join "the international family". This new republic had to do that so that it could use that family's rules to fight for China's sovereign rights and reject the "unequal treaties" that the Great Powers had imposed on them in the nineteenth century.[13]

The PRC after 1949 purported to scorn the system that excluded it for more than two decades. But, since its admission as the sole legitimate government of China into the inner circle of the UN Security Council in 1971, it has accepted that, whether called family or not, it could live with the United Nations structure around which the rest of the world turned. This did not mean that the Chinese agreed with all the assumptions that underpinned international law as understood in Europe and the United States. They had reservations about the universality of some of the assertions claimed in United Nations circles if only because they believed that some of them could lead to undue interference in what they considered to be a country's internal affairs. In addition, they knew their history and were conscious of alternative ways of dealing with the harsh realities in the power relations between polities.[14] For example, the loose term, family of nations, could provide more room for dealing with dynamic and unstable conditions while courts of international law could be appealed to as the last resort. They also recognized that there was room for improvement in the current international system and were ready to take part in moves to reform and improve that system as long as their views and interests were taken into account.

China has become deeply immersed in the UN processes since then, but many countries still ask what China really wants. Is it really committed to all the principles embodied in the UN Charter? Clearly the Chinese have learnt that nothing is absolute and immutable in power relationships. Therefore, international law can only be one of the means by which inequalities and uncertainties among nations are kept in check. Behind legalistic rules and practices have always been questions of humanity, morality and justice, and states dealing with one another needed to agree on the value systems that permitted constructive discourse before any rules could be seen as binding. In the meantime, the language of family and friendship helped to make the environment for negotiation and disputation less threatening. It is in that context that Chinese leaders and thinkers have abandoned the defined inequality of tributary relations in recognition of the dynamic realities of a globalized world. But, given the lack of enforceable laws, they have remained cautious about the fiction of equal sovereign states and have preferred the softer hierarchy implied in terms like family and friends among whom greater emphasis could be placed on ideas of reciprocity and moral responsibility. None of these have legal content, but they could enable necessary bilateral and multilateral relations, including those formalized by all varieties of treaties and agreements, to be conducted in a peaceful atmosphere while the international system was being improved. In short, nothing should be taken as final or sacred.

The Chinese world order described by John King Fairbank in the 1960s had been useful in Asia when all kingdoms and rulers believed in unequal relations and employed tribute-like feudal and personal language in their relationships. But the promise of the Westphalian system that acknowledged the sovereign rights of each state trumped that decisively, especially for smaller and weaker states.

When the Chinese were introduced to Wheaton's work on international law, they were greatly impressed by the way such law regulated the behaviour of the civilized nations and also justified the rights of a concert of powers that ruled over lesser peoples, including their imperial expansion and the acquisition of colonies. Dynastic officials compared these arguments with their own assumptions, centred on preserving the security and superiority of a single power. Where there was no such power centre but, instead, a number of competing powers, different rules and practices were needed. Hence the mandarins turned back to their ancient history, to the anarchic conditions in pre-Qin China during the period of the Warring States that were familiar to all Chinese scholars. They concluded that the modern global situation was a transitional state of affairs in which the challenge for hegemony could be bitter, painful and continuous, a view that still finds currency in Chinese analyses of the world situation today.[15] They also realized that China was in no position to join that challenge as long as it was technologically and economically inferior. When Japan not only defeated the Qing but also justified the war with the Wheatonian arguments that had guided the expansionist actions of other Great Powers, the Chinese were humiliated. By that time, Japan had been admitted into the family of nations as an equal while China was but a lowly family member with an "unequal" status that remained for another half-century.

In this context, family is an appropriate metaphor. There is generational inequality; there is stem and branch membership that mark degrees of relationships; and, among those of the same generation, there are older and younger siblings. Locating oneself within a family is something that the Chinese understood well. But they were alarmed when their country was treated as if it was a distant relative belonging to a weak branch, and in danger of being an older brother (possibly the eldest) only among the benighted natives of the European colonies.

How to recover the dignified position they once had and become a core member of the stem family of states became a matter that kept their best diplomats busy after 1895. But China's position continued to deteriorate despite their siding with the victorious allies during World War I. Joining the League of Nations, too, did not save it from losing control of (Outer) Mongolia and Manchuria, nor from another war with Japan that it had little hope of winning. Fortunately, the United States came into the war and, after 1945, catapulted China to Great Power status by insisting on having the Republic of China as one of the five Permanent

Members of the Security Council of the newly established United Nations. This provided the cockpit from which China could try to reposition itself. Ever since 1978, the PRC has systematically laid the foundations for Great Power status through determined economic reforms. Now that the reforms have proved successful and had their dramatic impact on the capitalist world, what does that do to its relations with its neighbours in Asia?

Two of the challenges China faced to its once-dominant position in Asia are pertinent to the question of family and friendship in foreign relations. The earlier challenge concerns what family and friend could mean to the Chinese when their country was weak. The later challenge evolved in stages as China recovered from war, civil war and the Cold War and reached its present position when wealth and power is accumulating but with enough unpredictability to arouse fears among some of its Asian neighbours.

The first challenge lasted for half a century till the reunification by the CCP in 1949. By the 1920s, most young Chinese had abandoned the traditional idea of a superior Chinese civilization. Instead, there was the growing appeal of nationalism, whether directed against the Western empires or specifically against Japan, and this began to turn a civilizational concept — that of *tianxia* (All under Heaven) — into analogies with the national empires of the Great Powers. Adopting the rhetoric of nation-state expansionism and in response to actual encroachments on Chinese lands — for example, cession of territories like Hong Kong and Taiwan and the blurring of endangered borderland territories like Manchuria, Xinjiang and Tibet — the idea of Chinese sovereignty became sacred.

The strong emotions generated found their way into nationalist textbooks from the 1920s to the 1950s in order to claim political rights over all lands that had a tributary relationship with imperial China, especially those in Southeast Asia like Vietnam, Laos and Burma. This was misguided. The ardent nationalists had little understanding of the tributary system. What had served as devices for trade, defence and diplomacy, as well as displaying cultural superiority, were reinterpreted by them to mean that these smaller neighbouring states were either territories owing allegiance to China, or were simply Chinese lands lost to foreign powers.[16] It was an example of the transfer of the language of international law and the rhetoric of national power to be used to assert the Chinese position towards its neighbours in Asia and is perhaps the most striking example of rationalization of positions that had moved from one of strength and confidence to one of helplessness and victimhood.

But when China became disunited and weak and embraced nationalism to overcome that, especially in the 1920s and 1930s, China found that it had neither family nor friend among its Asian neighbours. In any case, all were subject to foreign dominance (including Thailand, though it was formally independent) or actual colonial administration, so that, even if the indigenous nationalists in these colonies were sympathetic, they were unable to be of any help. The only exception was Japan, a Great Power that was newly aggressive on Chinese soil. Neither family nor friend, it was instead a dangerous enemy against whom China had to look outside Asia for help to defend itself. This was something that China had never had to do before. It had joined the family of nations on terms dictated by the West, and now it had to seek assistance as a feeble new member.

There was, in fact, no country that China could call a friend. Even the help that it did receive from other members of the family of nations were clearly self-interested, and China could not count on having any of that help for any length of time.[17] Given these circumstances, it was understandable that some

Chinese leaders should turn to the deliberate mobilization of popular nationalism. In this, the nationalists were inspired by the successes of Japan and post-Bismarckian and Nazi Germany. They felt that they had no choice but to follow their example in order to fight off multiple threats to the country, most notably those of Japanese territorial ambitions, Soviet Russian ideological subversion and, not least, the total control of China's economy by foreign business interests from Europe and the United States.

Modern nationalism is a two-edged sword. At the positive end, it helps to build a loyal citizenry for national unity and this could receive sympathy. At the opposite end, however, it is spurred by a sense of inferiority to emphasize the restoration of former greatness, and the strong emotions aroused would recognize no family or friend outside the country's borders. China's primary goal was the difficult task of unifying its peoples and this led to anachronistic depictions of an ancient "world order" to match the colonial claims of Western powers in Asia and elsewhere. Thus Chinese leaders turned to unjustified territorial claims to remedy China's disunity and weakness.

The most striking cases in the textbooks that I recall using as a schoolboy in the state of Perak (one of the Federated Malay States of British Malaya) in the 1930s listed Korea, Vietnam, Burma, Laos and Malaya as some of China's "lost *colonies*". It is a good example of how, in adopting a nationalistic response following successive humiliations, the Nanjing authorities came to speak the language, and thus acquire the face, of its worst enemies. Although understandable, this could be alarming to China's neighbours in Asia. Most Chinese, including those who were resident overseas, were new to such nationalism and their responses were uneven. As a result, both nationalist Guomindang (GMD) and CCP leaders and their fervent supporters both at home and abroad, when faced with Japanese expansion, intensified their propaganda against Japan to produce the patriotic commitment they needed. But there was an unavoidable contradiction in this position. The louder the nationalist calls to action, the greater the danger of rejection by other nations that did not share China's fears. The main remedy against the consequences of chauvinism and isolation was to use skilled diplomacy to make friends among those who had some common interests with China. This required acceptance and mastery of the prevailing international system. To do that, it was necessary to affirm China's membership in the family of nations and show commitment to its values in spite of the system's faults and weaknesses. In the end, China discovered that the narrow nationalist path was incompatible with any claim to represent a higher moral order in international affairs. That danger was not lost among GMD and CCP leaders during World War II. Both realized that they had to modify their nationalism if they wanted to win friends among the other powers and the only way to do that was to act as a good member of the family.[18]

The second challenge arose after the end of World War II when the reunited China under the CCP began to rebuild new strength from abysmal weakness. The Mao Zedong era from 1949 till 1976 was an idiosyncratic one that historians will continue to explore. But it left a very strong impression on China's Asian neighbours. Offering support to fraternal communist parties that tried but failed to overthrow post-colonial nationalist leaders did little to win friends for China. Standing up to the Russians might have appealed to some Chinese nationalists, but the ideological reasons for doing so were at best mystifying, not least to those in Asia, including leftist political leaders in Japan, who were friendly towards the Chinese revolution. In retrospect, the major contribution of Mao's Cultural Revolution to later developments was to have touched a diplomatic bottom where China had neither family nor reliable friend to turn to for help. China's position during those years served to show how dangerous it was to be almost totally isolated.[19]

During the Mao years, China was kept out of the United Nations family for the first twenty-two years and had to be content with the socialist family. Many had believed that revolutionary internationalism would replace the failed nationalisms of the previous decades. But they found that bending to the will of the Soviet Union was increasingly unbearable. The socialist family permitted Big Brother to intervene in another country's internal affairs in the name of ideological conformity. And fraternal differences could still lead to dangerous rival nationalisms that cut across family feelings.[20]

Fortunately for China, the world outside was changing fast. Numerous international organizations were established by the United Nations Organization, scores of new nations joined that UN family and continuous attempts were made to refine and extend the writ of international law. With rapid decolonization in Asia and Africa, many new members were added to the UN. With the help of many such members, China eventually regained its position in the enlarged family. The Chinese then set out systematically to master the rules and mores that guided the behaviour of legally equal nations. Among the lessons they learnt was to substitute friendly symbols between communist-socialist parties with those between family member states. Above all, they also learnt that international laws were not as clear or absolute as they were made out to be and that they could only be enforced with great difficulty. In that context, formal alliances and partnerships offered no real advantage. Instead, while laws were being disputed and debated, the cultivation of family and friendly relations among nations remained invaluable in the new international organizations.

Thus Deng Xiaoping, who had no illusions about international law, reversed course after 1979. He turned to maximum pragmatism, and set out to win friends in Asia and be a good citizen in the family of nations. He recognized that the economic development of China to restore health and strength to its devastated structures would need time and help from a peaceful environment that only the international system could provide. As a direct result, China's growth since the reforms after 1978 has been remarkable. A strong China now stands before its Asian neighbours for the first time in over a century. As these neighbours gaze at that phenomenal transformation, there is speculation whether China could some time in the future return to a modern and sophisticated version of tributary relationships, one that China might dress up in accordance with international relations theory. But the overall thrust so far is clear. China is proactive in economic relations and has given priority to making friends wherever it can, most notably and urgently in its neighbourhood. There is keen interest in a new regionalism that hinges on Southeast Asia, one that could also be called upon to help China deal with its sensitive relations with Japan and Korea as well as help its wish to bring Taiwan back into its fold.[21]

China's concerns today are practical. The danger is that, without ideals and ideology, the efforts to search for shared values that are rooted deeply in Chinese soil could, if crudely handled, lead its people back to the nationalism that left China without family and friends and thus damage the progressive image that China wants to project to the outside world. Now that China is strong again, it cannot afford to display the kinds of nationalism associated with expansionism and empires. The international system understands how national empires could lurk behind the rhetoric of national pride and it can normally check such developments among its smaller members. But the system cannot easily contain imperial urges when a country is large and strong. Thus the stronger China becomes, the more fearful its neighbours. If that strength were accompanied by nationalism, China would find it difficult to convince them of its best intentions. Chinese leaders have protested that they eschew nationalism and have no intention to expand in any direction. Their credibility depends on their ability to convince all concerned that China encourages economic growth only to satisfy the people's needs and arms itself only for defence. With consistent displays of friendship and family feeling expressed through self-control, strong civic discipline and respect for other people's values, a powerful China may actually help strengthen the international system that it has so cautiously embraced.

Notes

1. John K. Fairbank, ed., *The Chinese World Order: Traditional China's Foreign Relations* (Cambridge: Harvard University Press, 1968); Morris Rossabi, ed., *China Among Equals: The Middle Kingdom and its Neighbours, 10th–14th centuries* (Berkeley: University of California Press, 1983); Wang Gungwu, "Early Ming Relations with Southeast Asia, a Background Essay" in *Community and Nation: Essays on Southeast Asia and the Chinese* (Singapore and Sydney: Heinemann and Allen & Unwin, 1981), pp. 28–57, and "The Rhetoric of a Lesser Empire: Early Sung Relations with its Neighbours", in *The Chineseness of China: Selected Essays* (Hong Kong: Oxford University Press, 1991), pp. 100–17.

2. There is a vast literature debating such concepts since the publication of Wheaton's *Elements of International Law* in 1836. Particularly influential have been Hedley Bull, *The Anarchical Society: A Study of Order in World Politic* (London: Macmillan, 1977); and Robert Jervis, *Perception and misperception in international politics* (Princeton: Princeton University Press, 1976). A useful survey of some new issues is Michael Cox, Tim Dunne and Ken Booth, eds, *Empires, Systems*

and States: Great Transformations in International Politics (Cambridge: Cambridge University Press, 2001).

3. Fredrick McCormick, *The Flowery Republic* (London: John Murray, 1913), pp. 257–96. Duan Yunzhang, ed., *Sun Wen yu Riben shishi biannian*. 段云章.《孙文与日本史事编年》[Sun Yat-sen and Japan: A Chronological History] (Guangzhou: Guangdong Renmin Chubanshe, 1996), pp. 229–84; Li Jikui, *Sun Zhongshan yu Riben*, 李吉奎.《孙中山与日本》[Sun Yat-sen and Japan] (Guangzhou: Guangdong Renmin Chubanshe, 1996), pp. 286–303.

4. *Sun Zhongshan quanji* 《孙中山全集》[The Complete Works of Sun Yat-sen], vol. 2 (Beijing: Zhonghua shuju, 1982), pp. 1–19, 47–48, 94–97, 105, 160–67 and 316–29.

5. Zhang Weihua, *Mingshi Folangji Lusong Helan Yidaliya sizhuan zhushi* 张维华,《明史佛郎機呂宋和蘭意大里亞四傳注釋》[A Commentary of the Four Chapters on Portugal Spain Holland and Italy in History of Ming Dynasty] (Beijing: Hafo yanjing xueshe, 1934).

6. Fan Hong-ye, *Yesuhuishi yu Zhongguo kexue* 樊洪业,《耶稣会士与中国科学》[The Jesuits and Science in China] (Bei-jing: Zhongguo renmin daxue chubanshe, 1992); Fu, Lo-shu, ed., *A Documentary Chronicle of Sino-Western Relations, 1644–1820* (Tucson: The Association for Asian Studies by University of Arizona Press, 1966).

7. Xie Qinggao, *Hai Lu zhu* 谢清高,《海录注》[Annotated edition of Maritime Records] (Beijing: Zhonghua shuju, 1955); Wang Dahai, *Haidao yizhi jiaozhu*. 王大海,《海岛逸志校注》[Annotated Edition of Records and Anecdotes of the Island World] (Xianggang: Xuejin, 1992).

8. Lin Zexu, *Sizhou zhi* 林则徐,《四洲志》[Record of the Four Continents], annotated by Zhang Man 張曼 (Beijing: Huaxia chu ban she, 2002); Wei Yuan, *Haiguo tuzhi* 魏源,《海国图志》[Gazeteer and Maps of the Maritime World], annotated by Chen Hua et al. 陈华等 (长沙: 岳麓书社, 1998); Xu Jiyu, *Yinghuan zhilue jiaozhu*. 徐继畬,《瀛寰志略校注》[A Brief Description of the Ocean Circuit], annotated by Song Dachuan 宋大川 (Beijing: Wenwu chuban she, 2007).

9. Zhao Ersun deng, *Qingshi gao*. 赵尔巽等《清史稿》[Draft History

of the Qing Dynasty] (Changchun: Jilin chubanshe, 1995). On Korea, the edition stops with the Treaty of Shimonoseki (1895) and concludes by saying that Korea became fully independent. Other editions add that Korea was amalgamated with Japan. It also says that the Ryukyu kingdom ceased to exist. For Vietnam as for Laos, the sections conclude by saying that they came under the protection of the French. For Burma, the section notes that the British failed to send Burma's once-in-ten-years tribute due in 1898. For Siam, it points out how Siam remained independent between British and French colonies.

As for Sulu, it briefly mentions how the Spanish failed to subjugate the Muslim kingdom, and that it no longer sends tribute to the Qing emperor. Archival records show that that kingdom managed to sustain its tributary relations through the Qianlong emperor's reign (1736–95) despite several Spanish efforts to stop them; First National Archives, ed., *Qingdai zhongguo yu dongnanya geguo guanxi dang'anshiliao huibian*, 中国第一历史档案馆编，《清代中国与东南亚各国关系档案史料汇编》 [A Collection of Archives on the Relations between China and Southeast Asian Countries in Qing Dynasty], *Volume Two, The Philippines*. 《第二册，菲律宾卷》 (Beijing: International Cultural Publishing Co. 北京：国际文化出版公司).

10. Immanuel Hsu Chung-yueh completed his PhD thesis on China's entrance into the family of nations in 1954. This was subsequently published as *China's entrance into the family of nations: The diplomatic phase, 1858–1880* (Cambridge: Harvard University Press, 1960).

11. Odd Arne Westad, ed., *Brothers in arms: The rise and fall of the Sino-Soviet alliance, 1945–1963* (Washington, D.C.: Woodrow Wilson Center Press, and Stanford: Stanford University Press, 1998); Chen, Jian, *Mao's China and the Cold War* (Chapel Hill: The University of North Carolina Press, 2001).

12. See note 1.

13. Chinese diplomats had a very difficult time as the government visibly weakened after the Versailles Treaty in 1919. A good example of how the struggle to rid China of discriminatory parts of the

Unequal Treaties was seen at the time is Zeng Youhao, ed., *Zhongguo waijiaoshi* 曾友豪编, 《中国外交史》 [History of Chinese Diplomacy] (Shanghai: Commercial Press, 1926; reprinted as No. 187 of Part Two, *Jindai zhongguo shiliao congkan xubian* 《近代中国史料丛刊 续编》, 第十九辑, vol. 19, pp. 386–458). This may be compared with the work of later historians of Chinese foreign policies, for example, Wu Dongzhi, ed., 吴东之编, *Zhongguo waijiaoshi: Zhonghua minguo shiqi 1911–1949 nian* 《中国外交史:中华民国时期, 1911–1949 年》 [Diplomatic History of China: Republican Period, 1911–1949] (Henan: People's Publishing House, 1990), in which the unequal treaties debates during 1920–28 are covered on pp. 69–185. After the Nanjing government was established by the Guomindang in 1928, the nationalists briefly asserted themselves, but their efforts were totally undermined by the Japanese takeover of Manchuria three years later; Hong Junpei, ed., 洪钧培编. *Guomin zhengfu waijiaoshi* 《国民政府外交史》 [Diplomatic History of the Republican Government] (Shanghai: Huatong Publishing, 1932; reprinted as no. 280 *in Jindai zhongguo shiliao congkan* 《近代中国史料丛刊》 (Taipei: Wenhai Publishers, 1968)). For a broader perspective based on personal experience, see Gu Weijun, *Gu Weijun Huiyilu* 《顾维钧回忆录》 [The Memoirs of Wellington V.K. Koo] (Beijing: Zhonghua Publishing Co., 1983), vol. 1, pp. 316–65, 391–400, 409–42.

14. Alastair Iain Johnston and Robert S. Ross, eds., *Engaging China: The Management of an Emerging Power* (London: Routledge 1999), especially the essay by Alastair Iain Johnston and Paul Evans, "China's engagement with multilateral security institutions", pp. 235–71.

15. Richard L. Walker, The *Multi-state System of China* (Hamden, Conn.: Shoe String Press, 1954).

16. See chapter by Zheng Yangwen in *Negotiating Asymmetry: China's Place in Asia*, edited by Anthony Reid and Zheng Yangwen (Singapore: NUS Press, 2009).

17. The League's failure to deal with Japan's attack on Manchuria has left many documents and contemporary accounts. The most accessible record of the key issues is still W.W. Willoughby, *The Sino-Japanese*

Controversy and the League of Nations (New York: Greenwood Press, 1968 [first published in 1935]). Willoughby's perceptive conclusions are in pp. 657–69. S.R. Smith, *The Manchurian crisis, 1931–1932: A Tragedy in International Relations* (New York: Columbia University Press, 1948), pp. 225–62, captures the hopeless position of China most effectively.

18. The clearest turnaround in style and purpose may be found in the speeches and writings of Soong Mei-ling (Madame Chiang Kai-shek), *This is Our China* (New York: Harper, 1940). In comparison, Mao Zedong's story to Edgar Snow reflects an alternative voice of a tentative and tactical reconciliation, *Red Star over China* (London: Victor Gollancz, 1937).

19. Wang Gungwu, *China and the World since 1949: The Impact of Independence, Modernity and Revolution* (New York: St. Martin's Press, 1977), pp. 106–41.

20. Shen Zhihua, Yang Kuisong et al. 沈志华、杨奎松等编著, *Zhong Su guanxi shigang*, 《1917–1991 中苏关系史纲》 [A History of Sino-Soviet Relations, 1917–1991] (Beijing: Xinhua Publishers, 2007). The last straw was probably the Brezhnev doctrine as applied to Czechoslovakia in 1968. But as shown in Robert A. Jones, *The Soviet Concept of "Limited Sovereignty" from Lenin to Gorbachev: The Brezhnev Doctrine* (Basingstoke: Macmillan, 1990), the roots of that doctrine can be traced much further back.

21. The PRC closely studied the establishment of the ASEAN-10, completed in 1999, and concluded that ASEAN represents a regionalism that China could not only live with but also build on to enhance peace and stability in its southern neighbourhood. There was a major shift in policy from an emphasis on bilateral relations to an acceptance of multilateral diplomacy by treating ASEAN as a unitary organization with which China wanted close economic ties. Within two years, Premier Zhu Rongji had moved quickly towards the China-ASEAN Free Trade Agreement. The ASEAN perspective on this development is sensitively described in Rodolfo C. Severino, *Southeast Asia in Search of an ASEAN Community: Insights from the*

Former ASEAN Secretary-General (Singapore: Institute of Southeast Asian Studies, 2006). Also, Wang Gungwu, "China and Southeast Asia: the Context of a New Beginning", in *Power Shift: China and Asia's New Dynamics*, edited by David Shambaugh (Berkeley: University of California Press, 2006), pp. 187–204.

INDEX

Note: Page numbers followed by "n" denote endnotes.

A

Abdul Aziz Shah, Sultan, 163
ageing population, 134n1
alien (*pendatang*), 112
Alliance Party, 16, 32
"All Under Heaven", *tianxia*, 170, 180n6, 197
Aminuddin Baki, 57n6
Anderson, Ben, 176, 183n18
Angkor empire, 167, 175
anti-colonialism, 44
anti-imperialism, 15, 105
anti-Manchu sentiment, 86–87
ANZAC (Australia and New Zealand Army Corps), 22, 27
ASEAN (Association of Southeast Asian Nations), 14, 27, 207n21
Asia Research Institute, 3
Asian Tigers, 25
Australian Association of Asian Studies Conference, 11
Australian National University, 3, 7n2, 20, 63–64, 98

Australian Volunteers International, 147
Azahari, A.M., 14

B

Baba Peranakan, *see* Peranakan
Bandung Conference, 25
bangsa-centred bureaucracy, 50
Barisan National (BN), 48, 141
Batavia, massacre in, 80
Beiyang College, 186
Benda, Harry, 63
Berlin, Isaiah, 155
Boer War, 104
Book of Documents (*Shangshu*), 128
Brezhnev doctrine, 207n20
British colonies, 11, 29
British Commonwealth, *see* Commonwealth of Nation
British East India Company, 77, 79, 166, 173
British Empire, 6, 78–79, 104–05, 161–63, 169, 176

British empire and Commonwealth:
    A history for senior forms, The,
    180n5
British Empire Exhibition, 41,
    57n7
British India, 42, 145, 165
British Malaya, 37–39, 41–43, 52,
    82, 89, 100, 107, 159, 164,
    179n3, 199
    Chinese nation, and, 103–06
"brothers in arms", 192
Brunei Revolt, 14
bumiputera (sons of the soil), 30,
    112
Bush, George W., 148
business dealings, trust and, 125

C
Cambridge University, 179n3
capitalism, 6, 12, 45, 79, 169,
    175, 182n17
CCP (Chinese Communist Party),
    26, 106, 154, 164, 190–91,
    197, 199–200
centralization, 43, 45, 47, 49,
    52–53
Chan Heng Chee, 63–64, 67
"Changing identities of the
    Southeast Asian Chinese
    since World War II",
    conference, 98, 114n3
chauvinism, 109, 200
Cheah Boon Kheng, 3, 36
Chia Siow Yue, 67

Chiang Kai-shek, 164, 191
Chin Peng, 40
China
    alliance, forging, 191–92
    "Five-nation republic", 104
    history in, 127–34
    Peranakan, and, 80–83
    Republican period, 88–90
    tributary states, 189
    war against Japan, 128, 205n9
China and the World since 1949:
    The impact of independence,
    modernity and revolution, 7n2
China-ASEAN Free Trade
    Agreement, 207n21
"China Proper", 170
Chinese and the 1911 Revolution,
    with special reference to
    Singapore and Malaya, The,
    115n5
Chinese associations, 122
Chinese Communist Party,
    see CCP
Chinese empire, 159, 165, 167,
    170
Chinese heritage, and Singapore, 4
Chinese high school, 107
Chinese identity, 54, 71, 74–76,
    79–81, 85, 89, 97–99, 105,
    109–12, 114n2, 130
    Peranakan and, 84–92
"Chinese identity and loyalty in
    Singapore in the 19th and
    20th centuries", lecture, 97

Chinese in Malaya, The, 179n3
Chinese in Southeast Asia, The,
    179n3
Chinese nation, and British
    Malaya, 103–06
Chinese Peranakan, *see* Peranakan
Chinese secret societies in Malaya:
    A survey of the Triad Society
    from 1800 to 1900, 115n4
Chinese Singapore, 111–14
Chinese society in 19th century
    Singapore, 115n4
Chinese surnames, 121–22,
    135n7
Chinese Totok, 81–83
"Chinese world order" 170,
    181n14, 184, 192
Christianity, 151
"Christians and gold", 173, 173
Chunqiu (Spring and Autumn
    Annals), 128
Church and State, 152
citizenship rights, 11, 45
civil war, 2, 88, 107, 145, 164–55,
    180n9, 187, 197
class division, 16
class war, 21
Clifford, Hugh, 41, 57n7
Coedes, Georges, 166, 181n12
Cold War, 12, 24–25, 27, 36, 65,
    106, 177, 197
Colley, Linda, 176, 183n18
colonialism, 44, 54, 124, 143,
    161

Comber, Leon, 115n4
Commonwealth of Nations, 22,
    28, 40, 176, 162, 169, 176,
    180n5
communal politics, 16, 20–21,
    23, 37, 40, 106
communal tension, 46, 144
communism, 3, 5, 12, 15, 24–25,
    109, 128
confrontation policy, *see*
    Konfrontasi
Confucian Classics, 130
Confucian ethics, 6, 63, 104, 126
"Confucian merchant", 125
Confucius, 121, 123, 128, 130
constitutional monarchy, 20
constitutional rights, of Malay
    rulers, 45, 48
Cornell University, 142
corruption, 51
Covenant of the League of
    Nations, 191
cross-border identity, 92
Crusades, 173
Crush Malaysia (*"Ganyang*
    Malaysia"), 109, 142
cultural identity, 90, 108, 112
Cultural Revolution, 3, 7n2, 110,
    135n3, 200

D

Dai Viet kingdom, 175
Decline of constitutional democracy
    in Indonesia, 142

decolonization, 5, 12, 24, 27, 39,
    83, 109, 126, 139, 149, 160,
    163, 169, 201
    Southeast Asia, and, 83–84
"deimperialized", 163
Deng Xiaoping, 32, 68, 192, 202
Desker, Barry, 72n1
divergent policies, 141–46
"Divisive modernity", lecture, 5
Dutch East India Company,
    77–78, 173
Dutch revolt, against Spain, 78,
    95n6
dynastic system, end of, 130

E
East Asian Institute (EAI), 66–67
East Malaysia, 48–49
election, 15–16, 20–21, 50, 156n1
Elements of International Law, 193
Emergency, 20, 46–47, 54
Emerson, Rupert, 164, 180n8
Emperor's Four Treasuries, 130
Empire Day, 163
empires, end of, 159–79
endowment fund, 66
English East India Company, *see*
    British East India Company
English schools, 107

F
Fairbank, John King, 170, 192,
    195
Falungong, 151–54

"family of nations", 190–92, 194,
    200
Federated Malay States (FMS), 39,
    41, 199
    see also Unfederated Malay States
Federation of Malaya, 11, 14, 16,
    18, 23, 37–39, 45, 47–48, 51,
    55, 106
Federation of Malaysia, 20, 27,
    36–38, 61–62, 141–45
Feith, Herb, 5, 139–45, 147–49,
    151–52, 155
filial piety, 125
financial crisis, 51
First World War, *see* World War I
"Five-nation republic", 104
five tigers shrine, 115n4
"Former Ford Factory", 56n2
four categories of knowledge, 130
French empire, 175
French Enlightenment, 78
French Revolution, 78

G
Gadjah Mada University, 148
"*Ganyang* Malaysia" (Crush
    Malaysia), 109, 142
Gestapu coup, 26–27
globalization, 119, 150
Goh Keng Swee, 1–2, 4, 61–71,
    93n1
Goh Keng Swee: A Portrait, 71n1
*Goh Keng Swee: A Public Career
    Remembered*, 72n1

governance-centred heritage, 127
Great Leap Forward, 26
Great Peranakans: Fifty remarkable lives, 114n5
Great Powers, 79, 184–88, 190–91, 193, 196–98
Greater Malaysia, 4, 38
Greco-Roman tradition, 120
Gu Hongming, 87, 104
Guomindang (GMD), 82, 199–200, 206n13
guoyu, national language, 105
Gurney, Henry, 164

H
Haiguo tuzhi, 188
Hall, D.G.E., 175, 182n16
Han Chinese, 81, 86, 101, 104
Han dynasty, 130
hanjian (traitors), 112
Herb Feith Foundation, 139
"Heritage and History", lecture, 118
Heritage Science Conference, 118
History of Nation-Building Series, 67
Hobsbawn, Eric, 176, 183n18
Holy Book, 130
Holy Land, 173
Home Is Not Here, 7n1
Housing Development Board, 66
Hsu, Immanuel, 190
huaqiao (overseas Chinese), 82, 88–89, 103, 114n2

I
Identities of Southeast Asian Chinese since World War II, 114n3
identity, and loyalty, 4, 97–101
Illustrated Guide to British Malaya, 41, 57n7
immigrant states, 29
Imperial Catalogue, 130
imperialism, 13, 79, 105, 144, 166, 175, 182n17
In lieu of ideology: The intellectual biography of Goh Keng Swee, 71n1
Industrial Revolution, 77–78, 173
Inside Indonesia, 148
Institute of East Asian Philosophies, 64
Institute of East Asian Political Economy (IEAPE), 64–65, 67, 72n1
Institute of Southeast Asian Studies, establishment of, 62, 64, 67
"international family", 193
international law, 194–95, 201–02
Iranian revolution, 145
Iskandar Shah, Sultan, 163
Islam, 30, 50–51, 145–46, 150–51

J
Jackson, James C., 3, 11
Jackson Memorial Lecture, 11

Japanese empire, 159–60, 163,
    167
Japanese occupation, 39, 43–45,
    83, 105, 107, 126
Jesuits, 188

K
Kang Youwei, 115n5
Kesavapany, K., 67
Khoo Seok Wan, 115n5
kinship system, 127
Kissinger, Henry, 31
knowledge, four categories of,
    130
Konfrontasi, 13–14, 25–26, 142
Konfrontasi: The Indonesia-
    Malaysia dispute, 1963–1966,
    33n2
Kong family, 121
Korean War, 46
Koxinga, 172
Kwa Chong Guan, 72n1, 93n1

L
League of Nations, 191, 196
Lee Hsien Loong, 91
Lee Kam Hing, 93n1
Lee Kuan Yew, 17, 117n11, 143
Lee Poh Ping, 115n4
Legge, John, 63, 140, 147
Liddle, Bill, 14
Lim Boon Keng, 71, 87, 104,
    115n5
Lim Pin, 65–66

Lin Zexu, 188
lineage traditions, 121
lingua franca, 77
Long, Joey, 24
"Look East", 50
"lost colonies", 199
loyalty, and identity, 4, 97–101

M
Macartney, Lord, 188
Macgregor, Ian A., 181n10
Mackie, Jamie, 33n2, 147
Mahathir Mohamad, 57n6
Majapahit empire, 167, 174
Malacca Empire, 163, 167, 174,
    180n7
Malay Annals (Sejarah Melayu),
    180n7
Malay Archipelago, 17
Malay Land (Tanah Melayu), 15,
    37, 41, 47–52, 54
Malay Nationalist Party of
    Malaya, see PKMM
Malay power, 17, 23, 70
Malay rulers, constitutional rights
    of, 45, 48
Malaya
    capital and labour in, 42–43,
        45–46
    Singapore in, 38–41
    state, as a, 43–47
    see also Malaysia
"Malaya and New Paths to
    Nationhood", lecture, 36

"Malaya belonging to England",
    37
*Malaya: The Straits Settlements and
    the Federated and Unfederated
    Malay States*, 41
Malaya with Indonesia (Melayu
    Raya), 55n1
Malayan Chinese Association, 71
Malayan Communist Party, 14,
    40, 42, 46–47
Malayan identity, 61
Malayan People's Socialist Front,
    16
Malayan Union, 37–39, 41, 44,
    52, 56n4, 106
Malaysia
    break-up of, 148
    formation, 11, 37, 48
    nation building, 28
    Singapore separation from,
        2, 5, 20, 22–23, 28, 33,
        37–38, 41, 50, 52
    see also Malaya
Malaysia: A Survey, 13, 61–62
Malaysia Day, 19
Malaysia and Singapore Society
    of Australia, 3, 11
Malaysian Malaysia, 20–23, 29
Manchu, 80–81, 86–87, 101–04,
    124, 161, 172, 175, 187–88
Mao Zedong, 3, 7n2, 26, 31, 70,
    110, 191–92, 200–01, 207n18
maritime trade, 25, 67, 70, 168,
    174, 176

Marxist-Leninist doctrines, 130
May Fourth Movement, 105
Meiji Restoration, 189
Melayu Raya (Malaya with
    Indonesia), 55n1
meritocracy, 53–54
Ming dynasty, 7n2, 76, 130,
    182n14, 187, 188–89
Ming History, 188
Ministry of Education, 134n1
Ministry of External Affairs, 20
monarchy, 50–51
Monash University, 5, 139–40,
    142
Mongol, 104
mother tongue, 77
multicultural society, 3, 29–31,
    39, 53, 109, 126, 128, 144,
    148
Muslim Hui, 104

N
Nanhai (South China Sea), 7n2
"Nanhai trade, The", 182n16
Nanyang (South Seas)
    Communist Party, 41
Nanyang Technological
    University, 118
Nanyang University, 108, 117n9
Nanyang University Curriculum
    Review Committee, 62, 72n3
Napoleonic wars, 53
nation building, beginnings of,
    94n6

National Central University, 2, 164

national empire, 82, 166, 170, 174–77, 182n17, 197, 202

Peranakan living in, 77–80

National Front, *see* Barisan National

National Heritage Board, 118

national identity, 75, 79, 89, 93, 105, 109–13, 133

National Library, 97–98

National Library Prominent Speaker Series, 97

national religion, 146

nationalism, 18, 30, 44–45, 47, 54, 71, 78, 81–88, 105, 107, 112, 126, 128, 197–203

Nationalist Party, 170

Nations and Nationalism, 94n6

native (*xiangtu*) culture, 101, 121

natural law, 193

neo-colonialism, 143, 161

neo-imperialism, 161

Netherlands East Indies, 88

New World, 29

NGO (non-governmental organization), 123, 149–50, 157n8

Nixon, Richard, 31

non-communal polity, 20

NUS (National University of Singapore), 3, 36, 62–67, 73 *see also* University of Singapore

O

Ohio State University, 148

One Hundred Years' History of the Chinese in Singapore, 97, 114n1

Ong Pang Boon, 62

Ooi Kee Beng, 71n1

opium trade, 174

Our Place in Time: Exploring heritage and memory in Singapore, 134n1

overseas Chinese (*huaqiao*), 82, 88–89, 103, 114n2

Owyang, Hsuan, 66

P

Pancasila doctrine, 151

Pan-Malayan Islamic Party (PMIP), *see* PAS

PAP (People's Action Party), 17–18, 24, 69, 141

Parkinson, Cyril Northcote, 165, 174

PAS (Parti Islam Se-Malaysia), 16, 146

patriotism, 107, 109

pendatang (alien), 112

People's Liberation Army, 2

Peranakan, 4, 17, 71, 73–76, 80–81, 83–84, 99, 104–05, 114n1, 123–24, 126

Chinese identity, and, 84–92

early Singapore, in, 101–03

national empires, living in, 77–80
nationalistic China, and, 80–83
pre-national origins, 76–77
Peranakan Association, 74, 91
Peranakan Chinese in a Globalizing Southeast Asia, 73
Peranakan Museum, 74, 91
Peranakan phenomenon, 75–76, 85, 93
PKI (Parti Kommunis Indonesia), 25, 27, 110
PKMM (Parti Kebangsaan Melayu Malaya), 55n1
plural society, 20, 42, 48, 50, 52–54, 101, 108–09, 112, 126
political engineering, 22
political exiles, 107
political identity, 44, 106
post-national identity, 85, 92
pribumi, 48
proto-national community, 75–76, 83, 86
proto-national identity, 84, 87
Purcell, Victor, 162, 179n3

Q
Qianlong Emperor, 188, 205n9
Qin-Han Empire, 129, 171
Qing dynasty, 7n2, 70, 76, 80, 85–88, 101–03, 124, 161, 188–89
qigong, 153

R
racism, 124
Radio Sarawak, 114n2
Raja Bendahara, 163
Red Guards, 135n3
Reframing Singapore: Memory — Identity — Transregionalism, 115n3
regionalism, 202, 207n21
republicanism, 18
Revolution of 1911, 81
riots, 20, 50, 54, 142
Roman Empire, 78–79, 162
Royal Asiatic Society, 3, 36, 41
ruler-subject relationship, 123
Russian Empire, 177
Ryukyu islands, 189, 205n9

S
Sabah, 12, 17, 19, 21–24, 29, 37, 47–49, 144
"sacred sites", 135n3
Sandhu, Kernial Singh, 63
Sarawak, 12, 17, 19, 21–24, 29, 37, 47–49, 144
SEATO (Southeast Asia Treaty Organization), 24
Second World War, *see* World War II
secret "brotherhoods", 102
secret society, 86, 100, 102
secular divide, 151–55
secularism, 54, 151–53

Sejarah Melayu (Malay Annals), 180n7
self-government, 44
September 30 Movement, 26, 110
shi-history, 128–31
Short History of the Nanyang Chinese, A, 114n2
shuguo (tributary states), 189
Siamese empire, 167, 175
Silverstein, Josef, 63
Singapore
    Chinese heritage, and, 4
    heritage in, 119–27
    identity, 113
    Malaya, in, 38–41
    nation-state, global city, 107–11
    Peranakan in, 101–03
    separation from Malaysia, 2, 5, 20, 22–23, 28, 33, 37–38, 41, 50, 52
Singapore Chinese, 111–14
Singapore Chronicles, 136n11
Singapore Heritage Society, 134n1
Singapore problem, 19
Singapore story, 124
sinkheh, 81, 87–89, 99, 102
Sino-Indian relations, 25
Sino-Indonesian relations, 31–32
Sino-Japanese War, 71
Sino-Soviet Treaty of Friendship, Alliance and Mutual Assistance, 192
Sizhou ji, 188
Snow, Edgar, 207n18

socialism, 27, 154
"soft power", 30
Song dynasty, 122, 130, 171
Song Ong Siang, 97, 114n1, 115n5
sons of the soil (*bumiputera*), 30, 112
Soong Mei-ling, 207n18
South Seas (Nanyang) Communist Party, 41
Southeast Asia, and decolonization, 83–84
"Southeast Asia: Past, present and future", conference, 159–60
Southeast Asia Treaty Organization (SEATO), 24
Southeastern University, 159
Soviet Union, 14, 25–26, 30, 106, 177, 191–92, 201
Spain, Dutch revolt against, 78, 95n6
Special Economic Zones, 64
Spring and Autumn Annals (*Chunqiu*), 128
Sri Vijaya empire, 167–68, 174
state-system, 193
Stokes, Eric, 165
Straits Chinese, *see* Peranakan
Straits Chinese Magazine: A Quarterly Journal of Oriental and Occidental Culture, The, 115n5
Straits Settlements, 11, 15, 17, 38, 42–43, 53, 73, 82, 124–25

"Study of Chinese Identities in Southeast Asia, The", 114n3
Suharto, 26, 31, 67, 140, 149
Sukarno, 5, 12–13, 24–27, 30, 32, 67, 109, 142–43
Sultan of Brunei, 18, 24
Sulu, 189, 205n9
Sun Yat-sen, 81–82, 87–88, 104, 115n5, 130, 170, 186–87, 191, 193
surname genealogy, 121–23
surname organizations, 122–23
Suryadinata, Leo, 73, 91
Swettenham, Frank, 41, 57n7
Syonan-to, 39, 52, 56n2

T
Taiping Rebellion, 87, 102
Taiwan, 25, 108, 110, 170, 172, 189, 193, 197, 202
Tan Cheng Lock, 71, 73, 84, 93n1
Tan Kah Kee, 88, 104, 107, 116–.6
Tan Keng Yam, Tony, 66
Tan Siew Sin, 69
Tan Siok Sun, 69, 71n1
Tanah Melayu (Malay Land), 15, 37, 41, 47–52, 54
Tang dynasty, 171
Tarling, Nicholas, 5–6, 159, 160–62, 164–66, 169, 173–74, 176, 178
Taylor, Keith, 182n16
Temple of Confucius, 135n3

Tenney, C.D., 186
terrorism, 148, 150
think-tank, 65
Thirteen Colonies, 29
Three Principles of the People, 130
tianxia, "All Under Heaven", 170, 180n6, 197
Tibetan, 104
Tongmeng Hui, 187
Totok Chinese, 81–83
Trade in the Eastern Seas, 1793–1813, 174
trade union, 46
traitors (*hanjian*), 112
Treaty of Friendship and Alliance, 191
Treaty of Pangkor, 103
Treaty of Shimonoseki, 205n9
tributary states (*shuguo*), 189
tributary system, 166, 185, 187–88, 192–93, 197–98
trust, and business dealings, 125
Tun Razak, 31
Tunku Abdul Rahman, 11–12, 17, 21, 38, 142, 145

U
UMNO (United Malays National Organization), 17, 20, 50, 146
"unequal treaties", 193, 206n13
UNESCO, 119, 133
Unfederated Malay States, 41, 43
see also Federated Malay States

United Nations, 31, 117n9, 184,
    191, 194, 201
United Nations Security Council,
    192, 194, 197
University of Auckland, 159
University of Hong Kong, 63–64
University of Malaya, 11–12, 20,
    39, 61, 70, 140, 165
University of Singapore, 62, 109
    see also NUS
University of West Sydney, 11

V
Versailles Treaty, 205n13
Victorian imperialism, 165
Vietnam, as proto-nation, 175,
    182n16

W
Wang Chonghui, 186
Wang Dahai, 188
War in the Eastern Seas, 1793–
    1815, 174
war of independence, 79
warlords, 88
Warring States, 195
Wealth of East Asian Nations, 71n1
Wei Yuan, 188
West Malaysia, 48
Wheaton, Henry, 193, 195–96
Williamson, James A., 180n5

Winstedt, Richard, 41, 57n7
Wolters, Oliver, 166, 168, 181n12
Wong, John, 64–66
"world order", 199
World War I, 191
World War II, 1, 3, 18, 38, 56n4,
    83, 98, 126, 161, 177, 200

X
Xiamen University, 88
xiangtu (native) culture, 101, 121
Xie Qinggao, 188
Xu Jiyu, 188

Y
Yen Ching-hwang, 115n5
Yeo, George, 67
Yinghuan zhilue, 188
Yongle, emperor, 171
Yuan dynasty, 171
Yuan Shikai, 186–87, 191

Z
Zhang Tingyu, 188
Zheng Chenggong, 172
Zheng He, 171
Zheng Yongnian, 66
Zhonghuaminzu, 104
Zhou Enlai, 31
Zhu Rongji, 207n21
Zhuang Qinyong, 115n4

ABOUT THE AUTHOR

Professor WANG Gungwu is National University of Singapore (NUS) University Professor and Emeritus Professor of Australian National University (ANU).

His recent books include *Diasporic Chinese Ventures: The Life and Work of Wang Gungwu* (2004); *Divided China: Preparing for Reunification, 883–947* (2007); *Renewal: The Chinese State and New Global History* (2013); and *Another China Cycle: Committing to Reform* (2014). His dialogues on world history were edited by Ooi Kee Beng, *The Eurasian Core and Its Edges* (2015). His latest book is *Home Is Not Here* (2018).

He received his BA Honours and MA from University of Malaya in Singapore and his PhD from SOAS, University of London. He was Professor of History at the University of Malaya (1963–68); Professor of Far Eastern History (1968–86) and Director of Research School of Pacific Studies at ANU (1975–80). In 1986–95, he was Vice-Chancellor of Hong Kong University. From 1996, he was Professorial Fellow at the Institute of Southeast Asian Studies (ISEAS; 1996–2002); Director of the East Asian Institute, NUS (1997–2007); and Chairman of the Lee Kuan Yew School of Public Policy (2005–17), the East Asian Institute (2007–18) and the ISEAS – Yusof Ishak Institute Board (since 2002).

www.ingramcontent.com/pod-product-compliance
Lightning Source LLC
Chambersburg PA
CBHW050212270326
41914CB00003BA/378